What Everyone Needs to Know about Tax

What Everyone Needs to Know about Tax

An Introduction to the UK Tax System

James Hannam

WILEY

Library of Congress Cataloging-in-Publication Data is available

ISBN 9781119375784 (pbk) ISBN 9781119375807 (ePDF)
ISBN 9781119375814 (ePub) ISBN 9781119375821 (obk)

Cover Design: Wiley
Cover Image: © White Lace Photo/Shutterstock

Set in 10/13 SabonLTStd by SPi Global, Chennai, India

Printed in Great Britain by TJ International, Padstow, Cornwall

10 9 8 7 6 5 4 3 2 1

To
Bart Invictus

Contents

About the author

James Hannam is a graduate of the universities of Oxford and Cambridge. He has worked as a tax advisor for 20 years at several City of London institutions including KPMG, Barclays Bank and Freshfields. For the last eight years he has been with EY. He lives in Kent with his wife and two children.

By the same author:
God's Philosophers: How the Medieval World Laid the Foundations of Modern Science

Introduction

Why you should read this book

You pay a lot of tax. Of course, you know that. But I bet you don't know just how *much* you pay or all the ways the government has to extract the cash from you. I think that's something you really need to know. It will make you into a better-informed voter who can see through the cant of politicians and the distortions in the media. I'm not asking whether we should pay more or less tax. I am saying that, even before we can answer that question, we have to understand about the tax we pay already.

By the end of this book, I hope you'll also see why with tax, as with so much in life, there are no straightforward solutions. We can't raise huge amounts of money just by taxing high earners and multinational companies, or by closing loopholes and chasing tax evaders. Were it that simple, the government would already be doing it. So, if we want the NHS, state education, a half-decent army and a welfare state, we just have to cough up. No one else is going to do it for us.

Before we start, an important word of warning: this book is *not* intended to help you pay less tax. A common version of the UK tax code, containing the law and various pieces of official guidance, is about 24,000 pages long. On top of that, there are at least 82 volumes of court decisions going back to 1875 and reams of material from the UK's tax authority, HM Revenue & Customs (usually abbreviated to HMRC). This book only has about 160 pages and the print is rather larger than in the standard edition of the legislation. That means you should not, under any circumstances, take action in respect of your tax affairs on the strength of what you read in these pages. No really, don't. It would be like attempting cosmetic surgery with only the expertise that you have gleaned from reading *The Silence of the Lambs*. Whether you are running a large company or living off a modest pension, you owe it to yourself to get some decent tax advice before risking any money. Even when I make some apparently definitive statement in these pages on, for example, ISAs or the VAT treatment of Jaffa Cakes, please don't take it at face value. The UK tax system is so unfeasibly complex, so Byzantine in its intricacy and changes so quickly, that even the simplest rules can have a dozen exceptions. In short, the purpose of this book is to help you become a more knowledgeable taxpayer and voter, not to save you money.

Income taxes

Let's look at some of the taxes you pay. If you are a worker, your employer will have been deducting tax and national insurance contributions from your pay packet each month and paying it directly over to the government. There's more: your employer also has to pay national insurance contributions on top of that. That's in addition to the national insurance that you pay. For a worker on an average wage of £26,500 a year, all those taxes comes to almost £8,000 a year: an effective tax rate on earnings of 30%. You probably know the basic rate of income tax is 20%, so you might be surprised to hear the effective tax rate for an average voter is rather higher than that, even taking into account the tax-free annual allowance. Of course, this is for workers on £26,500. If you are lucky enough to earn more, your effective tax rate will be even higher.

The cunning thing is the way the government collects all this tax. You earn the money, but the government diverts its share into the Treasury's coffers before you ever get your hands on a penny. The system of Pay As You Earn (usually abbreviated to PAYE) means you can be taxed without ever feeling it. It's a pernicious regime because it means you don't appreciate just how much you are paying. Imagine if you had to write a cheque to HM Revenue & Customs every month for hundreds of pounds. At the very least, you'd be demanding better value for money from public spending.

Since the largest element of taxation is on earnings and income, that's what we'll look at in Chapter 1 of this book. We'll be asking whether high earners contribute their fair share and see how tax traps the low paid in poverty.

Taxes on spending

Tax doesn't stop there, of course. Once you have what is left of your salary in the bank, you might want to spend it. Most purchases attract Value Added Tax, or VAT.

Let's combine several taxes into an everyday situation. Your young son has set his heart on a Lego truck for his birthday. There is a big articulated lorry available, guaranteed to flutter the heart of any small boy. The local toyshop would be delighted to sell this Lego set to you for £40, but it's obliged to add 20% VAT. Unfortunately, you've already had to pay income tax and national insurance on the money you need to pay the shopkeeper. As an average earner, to have the money in your pocket to buy the truck, you need to earn a grand total of £60 before any taxes. That's half again more than the basic cost of the Lego and it doesn't even include employers' national insurance.

You can see what's happening here. Lots of different taxes – income tax, employers' and employees' national insurance contributions and VAT – accumulate without the government ever having to admit what the total amount of pain is going to come to. Keeping the tax system complicated suits the government and, if I'm honest, it suits tax accountants like me as well. That's not because accountants are all helping their clients avoid taxes, it is just that calculating what you owe is so difficult that even the smallest of businesses need professional help to get it right.

VAT is an example of a tax that the government tries to keep invisible. When we look at a price tag, it already includes the VAT. The way taxes are collected through PAYE and the VAT system makes sure that, as an individual earner, you rarely have to hand over any money yourself. It is all done for you by your employer and businesses. The happy result (for the Treasury, at least) is that none of us have the foggiest how much tax we actually pay. That means, to some extent, all taxes are 'stealth taxes'.

There are no taxes quite so stealthy as the so-called green taxes pushing up our heating bills. Nonetheless, increase any tax enough and people start to notice. You may remember the fuel protests back in 2000. These were sparked off by increases of the duty on petrol and diesel.

Chapter 2 of this book is all about VAT, excise duties and green taxes: the taxes you pay on spending. We'll also see how tax gets in the way of free and fair trade, especially if you are a Third World farmer trying to sell your produce into the European Union.

And yet more taxes

As well as raising money, the government likes to use the tax system to encourage what it sees as virtuous behaviour. For example, it wants to promote thrift and provides incentives for us to save. We'll look at ISAs, pensions and other tax-efficient ways of locking your money away in Chapter 3. However, all these encouragements for us to save mean that the idle rich, who already have plenty of money in the bank, can get away with paying very low taxes indeed. They don't even need to resort to complicated avoidance schemes or to become a tax exile.

Capital gains tax applies on profits you make from investing in shares and other assets. Admittedly, you don't have to pay capital gains tax on your main residence when you sell it. But you do have to pay stamp duty when you buy your house, not to mention inheritance tax when you die in it. There is also council tax while you are living there, whether you own your home or not. We'll look at all these taxes on property in Chapter 3 as well.

Taxes on businesses

Company taxation has become a vexatious question. Are multinational companies like Google and Starbucks paying their fair shares? It sometimes seems that if the government went after them, the rest of us would have to pay a lot less.

It's true that some multinationals pay little tax in the UK, and the rules have recently been tightened up to deal with this. Remember, though: Google and Starbucks are American corporations so they should pay most of their tax in the USA. In any case, if we tax companies more, that doesn't let ordinary people off the hook. They still end up paying because company taxes are stealth taxes too. Companies all have customers, employees and shareholders. If you have a pension, life insurance policy or an ISA, you probably own shares in some big companies. Any tax on business has to be passed on to real people, so taxing companies is just another way of taxing you, but several levels removed so you are largely unaware of it. In Chapter 4, I'll clear up some of the common misconceptions about corporation tax and explain why many economists now realise that business taxes should be kept as low as possible.

That said, the international tax system is way behind the times. In the modern globalised economy of e-commerce and the internet, ideas (called 'intellectual property' in the jargon) are the most valuable things around. But because they are so mobile, taxing ideas is hard work. In Chapter 4, we'll also look at how governments have offered tax breaks for intellectual property to stay put, and how multinationals can move it around the world to keep their tax bills down. Luckily, in the last couple of years, there has been an international effort, initiated by the British government, to ensure that multinationals pay the right amount of tax.

Avoiding taxes

With all these taxes around, it is hardly surprising that some people try so hard to avoid paying them. But this is not often a good idea. The taxman is likely to take you to court if he thinks you are playing the system. And the courts are not sympathetic towards tax avoiders. At least tax avoidance is only likely to cost you money. Tax evaders can end up in prison. By the way, evasion and avoidance are very different beasts. If you evade taxes, you are using fraud to pull the wool over the taxman's eyes. It's illegal and you could be prosecuted. Tax avoidance means using clever ideas to exploit loopholes in the law. It's legal but opinion is divided on the extent to which it is morally defensible. Tax planning is doing what you would have done anyway (if tax wasn't a consideration) but doing it in a way that means you pay less tax. In many cases, the government encourages us to do this because it wants to incentivise certain kinds of behaviour. Most people consider tax planning acceptable, especially when they are doing it themselves. Few of us want to voluntarily pay more tax than we have to. Having a personal pension or an ISA are both examples of sensible planning. That said, the boundary between avoidance and planning is subjective. Not everyone agrees about where it is. Chapter 5 looks at these issues in more detail.

Avoidance is possible because the tax system is awesomely complicated. But simplifying things is much harder than you would hope. So, we'll wind up the fifth chapter by looking at why tax reform is so difficult and why the law is so convoluted.

I started working as a tax accountant over 20 years ago. During the intervening period, I have had the privilege of advising some of the most prestigious and exciting companies in the world. However, you won't read about any of them in these pages. Rather than risk inadvertently giving away confidential information (or even appearing to do so when I haven't), I've steered clear of my own clients. The information in this book is either publicly available or an inference based on what's publicly available. By that, I mean material you can find on the internet (if you know where to look) or in published books. Where I have discussed real-world examples, I've done my best to verify what I've said through official documents. Facts and figures given in the text are current as at 1 January 2017.

I'd like to thank Jonathan Richards, Christopher Barton, Andrew Drysch, Rachel Phillipson and, most of all, my wife Vanessa for their helpful comments on the manuscript. Any remaining errors are entirely my responsibility. Thanks also to John Grogan as well as to Stephen Mullaly and his team at Wiley for all their hard work in turning this book into a reality.

Finally, all the opinions expressed in this book are mine alone. I don't expect that anyone will agree with all of them.

What Everyone Needs to Know about Tax

Taxes on your income and earnings

Income tax and national insurance

Income tax: when you think about tax, that's probably the tax you're thinking about. It was introduced by the Prime Minister, William Pitt the Younger, as a temporary measure in 1798 to fund the Napoleonic Wars. Legally, it's still temporary. Every year, Parliament has to vote for income tax to apply for another twelve months. If ever MPs failed to do so, the government would run out of money and have to shut down.

We all know that the basic rate of income tax is 20p in the pound and the higher rate is 40p. These headline figures are the UK's 'marginal rates of tax'. When tax experts talk about the marginal rate of tax, they mean the rate you pay on each extra pound of income that you earn. Just looking at income tax, the first £11,000 you earn is tax free so the marginal rate up to this amount is nil. Then it increases to 20%, the basic rate. When you earn over £43,000 the marginal income tax rate goes up to the higher rate of 40%. So, if you are paid £20,000 a year, your marginal income tax rate is 20% because if your pay increases to £20,001, you have to pay 20p of income tax on the extra pound you earn.

A 20p marginal rate of income tax doesn't sound so bad compared to all the public services we enjoy, like healthcare and education. But you have to factor in employers' and employees' national insurance as well. These add 26p of tax on each extra pound a basic rate taxpayer earns.

On top of that, any welfare benefits received from the government are reduced as we earn more. Handing back your benefit payments acts like yet another form of taxation on each extra pound you earn. For the lower paid, the way that benefits are phased out as people start working means they can face marginal tax rates of up to 90%. We'll talk some more about that later in the chapter. For the middle classes, child benefit is clawed back if anyone in the family earns over £50,000. Having to pay back child benefit has the same effect on take-home pay as an increase in tax. This means income tax and national insurance, together with benefit payments, can combine to produce very high marginal tax rates.

In the Introduction, I showed how you probably need to earn £60 to buy a Lego truck worth £40, once you include income tax, national insurance and VAT. That's £20 in taxes. However, this amount factors in your personal allowance of £11,000 on which you don't have to pay income tax. Now imagine you needed to work some overtime before you could afford to buy the toy. You've already used up your personal allowance so you now have to look at your marginal tax rate to work out how long you need to work. As a basic rate income taxpayer, you would need to earn £70.60 in overtime to buy that £40 truck. Thanks to high marginal rates of tax, over £30 of the £70.60 that your employer pays you to work the overtime goes to the government. That's an overall tax rate of 43%. Add employers' national insurance and it's 50% (see Figure 1.1). If you are a higher rate income taxpayer, your combined tax rate for ordinary purchases is 58%.

The way multiple taxes add up to big bucks is my First Golden Rule of tax: lots of small taxes together combine to make large tax bills. Rather than hit us with a single massive demand that we can't help feeling bad about, the system is organised into lots of smaller levies that accumulate. There are lots of different taxes with lots of different names charged on lots of different things. But, in the end, you and I end up paying them all.

Whether a tax is levied on the companies we work for, or the shops we buy from, it all comes out of our pockets. That's my

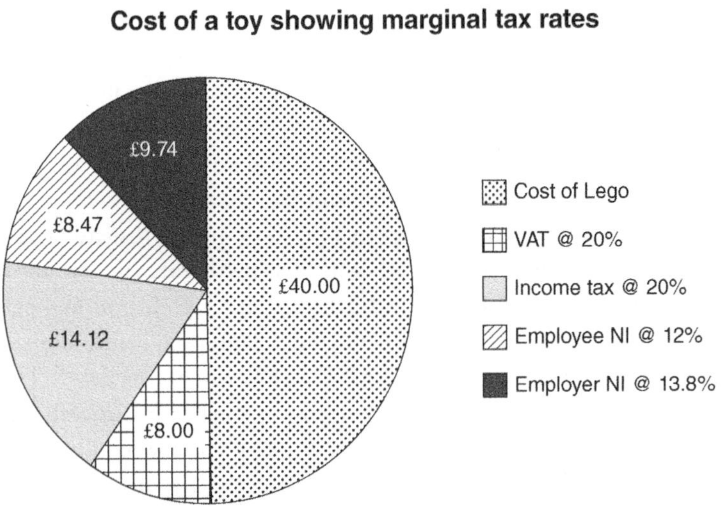

Cost of a toy showing marginal tax rates

Figure 1.1 The taxes on a £40 Lego set for a basic rate taxpayer showing taxes coming to as much as the toy.

Second Golden Rule of tax: no matter what name is on the bill, all tax is ultimately suffered by human beings. There is no magic pot of money for governments to dip into. Even when the government borrows, it must tax us in the future to pay back the debt. To understand your personal tax burden, you have to add up all taxes, even the ones that you don't pay directly and may not even know about.

National insurance contributions

We've seen that, as well as income tax, we also pay national insurance contributions on our salaries. It's time to have a closer look at this most misunderstood of taxes.

When you pay national insurance contributions (usually abbreviated to 'NICs'), what exactly are you contributing to? Many people are vaguely aware of a link between national insurance and their state pension. Indeed, you need to have been paying NICs for

30 years to qualify for the full state pension (if you miss a few years out, you can catch up on them later).

Let's see what that means. Assume you are on average earnings of £26,500 throughout your 35-year working life. That means the combined employees' and employers' national insurance contributions paid on your salary will be about £4,750 a year. Now, suppose you invested that £4,750 a year in a private pension instead of paying it over to the government. With a growth rate of 5% above inflation (the long-run rate of return for shares), your notional pension pot from payments equivalent to your national insurance contributions should be worth over £430,000 when you retire. That would get you an index-linked pension at today's historically low annuity rates of £14,750 a year. A few years ago it would have got you considerably more and, once interest rates return to normal levels with the economic recovery, we can expect pension annuity rates to rise as well. Alternatively, under the new pension freedom rules, you could take that £430,000 as income or reinvest it.

The £14,750 a year pension you would have from saving £4,750 a year in a private pension scheme is a much better deal than the state pension of £8,094 that you really get for making those 35 years of contributions. Worse, if you work for longer (as most of us do) or pay higher NICs because you have higher earnings, you don't get a better state pension. The government does pay our national insurance contributions into a special fund separate from general taxation. But it is not investing the money to pay for your pension when you retire. The national insurance fund only has enough money in it to pay for about two months of benefits for today's claimants. In essence, it is a current account, not a savings account. The government collects money from people currently in work to pay pensions to today's retirees. There is no money set aside to fund pensions in the future. We are entirely reliant on our children being willing to cough up in the same way we have. So, looked at as a contributory pension scheme, national insurance is a very bad deal. However, we should instead regard NICs as another income tax with a different name. It accounts for a fifth of the government's revenues. Although it funds pensions and some other benefits, a large amount of it is used to pay for the NHS. Now, of course, the NHS needs funding and our taxes are the way to do it. But given national insurance contributions have no real contributory element and are really a tax on earnings, why don't we call them a tax?

The answer is one of low politics rather than high principle. At the most basic level, it's a manifestation of the First Golden Rule of tax: lots of small taxes together combine to make large tax bills. It suits the government that we pay multiple taxes with low rates rather than a single transparent and easily understood levy. The complexity of the tax system means no one ever realises how much he or she is paying. This makes it a whole lot easier to extract more tax from us without causing a revolution. Combining income tax with employees' and employers' national insurance into a single levy would give us a basic rate of income tax of about 45p in the pound. No government wants to admit that tax rates are that high. So they prefer the sleight of hand of having a 20p income tax rate, 12% employees' national insurance contributions and the essentially invisible 13.8% employers' national insurance contributions.

What, you might ask, is the difference between employers' and employees' national insurance? In all honesty: nothing. They are both taxes on your salary, they are both collected in the same way (through PAYE, which we will discuss further below) and your employer sees them both as amounts they have to pay to keep you turning up to work. The main distinction is that earnings are capped at £43,000 when calculating most of an employee's NICs (and the version paid by the self-employed). This recognises that, by earning more, you don't get better benefits or a bigger pension from the system. In fact, it was not until the 1970s that national insurance stopped being charged at a flat rate so that everyone paid the same. Thanks to Gordon Brown, you now also pay 2% NICs on your earnings over the £43,000 threshold.

Employers' NICs are 13.8% of our entire salary above £8,112 without any upper limit. That means employers' national insurance embodies the Golden Rules of tax: following the First Rule, it is kept separate from income tax, even though it is a tax on income. This disguises just how much we actually pay. It is also in accordance with the Second Golden Rule: no matter what name is on the bill, all tax is ultimately suffered by human beings. Because this element of national insurance is paid by our employers, we don't realise that we are suffering it. But, despite all the subterfuge, ordinary people still end up shelling out.

If you are in work, it's a good rule of thumb to treat NICs and income tax as the same thing, although there are, inevitably, various wrinkles and complications in the rules. For example, savers and pensioners pay income tax but not national insurance. When you factor in employers' NICs, this means there is twice as much tax on wages from work than on money you get from savings or your pension. This might make sense economically, since we do want to encourage saving. And maybe it is fair that pensioners, after being taxed all their lives, don't have to keep paying national insurance after they've retired. But that doesn't explain why wealthy pensioners are taxed a great deal less than low-paid workers.

In most respects, however, NICs and income tax are drawing ever closer together. For example, until 1991, there was no national insurance on many perks such as company cars. Even in the 1990s, it was still possible to exploit gaps between the rules on income tax and NICs. Some city firms were paying bonuses in gold or diamonds to avoid national insurance (which was payable on cash wages only).

More recently, both Labour and Conservative governments have been ironing out the smaller wrinkles to make national insurance and income tax as similar as possible. Nowadays, many benefits in kind, including company cars, are subject to both income tax and employers' national insurance. They go on a special form called a P11D and you pay tax on the monetary value of a benefit as if it were cash. As it happens, one of the most tax-efficient perks available today is not turning up to work. If you take extra holiday as a benefit (and many firms allow their employees a few extra days a year in exchange for sacrificing some of their salary), the cost to you is only the pay you would have received after tax.

Although income tax and NICs are now administratively almost identical, no politician is going to amalgamate them into a single transparent rate of tax. After all, under the First Golden Rule, there is no sense in emphasising how high the combined rates of tax that we pay really are. Tory MP Ben Gummer did suggest in 2014 that NICs should be renamed 'earnings tax'. That would, at least, be a candid name.

Paying tax

Most people with jobs don't have to worry about paying their taxes as it is all done for them automatically. Payslips show the tax paid, but many of us never really look at any figure except the bottom line, which is our take-home pay. We pay most of our taxes through PAYE, which was invented at the end of the Second World War as a way to improve the efficiency of tax collection. From the point of view of the government, it has three major advantages. The first is the official one. The administration of the tax system for employees was handed to the people they work for. It was no longer necessary for individual workers to figure out how much tax to pay. Instead, our employers calculate the tax we owe and deduct it from our salary. We only ever receive our net wages. The tax component is paid straight over to HMRC. In effect, this privatised a large chunk of tax collection. The primary responsibility for gathering tax was transferred from the tax authority to employers. They bear the cost and suffer the penalty if things go wrong. It is much easier for HMRC to audit employers' tax collection systems than it is to check the tax returns of all the individual employees.

The second advantage of PAYE for the government is that it accelerates when the money arrives in the Treasury's coffers. With PAYE, the government gets paid monthly, just like we do. I receive my net salary and the Exchequer receives both the income tax and national insurance. Given that, between them, NICs and income tax collected through PAYE account for over half the government's total tax-take, the cash flow benefits of regular payment are extremely significant.

The third advantage of PAYE is the subtlest, but perhaps the most important: we never see the tax we are paying. Out of sight, it is kept out of mind. Employers' NICs are also concealed in plain sight. Most of us never think about them or realise that they are a tax on our salary just as much as income tax. Even though employees' national insurance and income tax are supposedly taxes that we pay ourselves, the system requires businesses to pay these taxes on our behalf using the same PAYE machinery with which they account for employers' national insurance. So we never possess our money before the government gets its paws on it.

Ensuring that we hardly ever have to pay any tax directly is a major pillar of the UK's revenue system. In fact, it is a principle that deserves to be enshrined in the Third Golden Rule of tax: taxes are kept as invisible as possible. The government wants to avoid people paying their taxes directly so they are less likely to notice them. I can explain why this is so important from personal experience.

As I noted in the Introduction, I've worked as an accountant for many years. But I'm also occasionally paid for my journalism. This means I have to fill out a tax return each January. Completing the return is a pain, but nothing like as painful as what happens next. Once I've calculated my tax bill for the year, I have to write a cheque for what I owe. This is not usually very large, a few hundred pounds in most years, occasionally a couple of thousand. But I resent writing that cheque far more than I do paying the tax on my regular salary, even though the latter is a much greater amount. I also have to make sure I've saved up enough to cover the bill. Seeing the money leave my bank account and sail off into the grateful arms of the Chancellor of the Exchequer seems far more onerous than the cumulatively much bigger deductions my employer makes from my monthly wages.

Under PAYE, most people don't have to fill out a tax return, let alone write a cheque to HMRC. We never receive the tax we pay on our salaries. This means we never feel its loss. In fact, although we all seem to know what our monthly take-home pay is, few can recall our monthly gross salaries. Surprisingly, many people aren't even sure exactly what their annual gross salary is. The pain of the tax being deducted at source is much less than if we received our salaries gross and then had to pay the tax ourselves.

In recent years, many businesses have done away with paper payslips, so employees have to go online to see them. Since we rarely do that, we've become even more remote from the taxes on our salaries. However, this is only the start of the digitisation process. HMRC has launched a grand project called Making Tax Digital that will require employers to use the PAYE machinery to deduct the tax we owe on our savings and other income, as well as on our salary. This is supposed to mean the annual tax return, still filled in by ten million of us, can be abolished by 2020. Without this one occasion each year when we have to face up to the amount we have paid, the distance between taxpayers and the tax collection machinery will grow to a chasm.

The distorting effect of PAYE is that we pay more tax than we feel like we do. This means we are less demanding than we should be about value for money from public spending. We are also less aware that increases in public spending are something that we all pay for. PAYE helps the government convince us the money it spends is somehow different from the money in our wallets and bank accounts. For example, we call the NHS and state education 'free' when they are really nothing of the sort.

Not that I think we should abolish PAYE. If we did, the country would go bust within weeks. But I do think it is important that taxpayers know how much they pay. The cumulative effect of the three Golden Rules of tax is that we put up with failures in the public sector that we would not tolerate in our own affairs. Surely we should expect the same value for our taxes as we do from the money we spend at our local supermarket. We also accept much higher levels of taxation than those that have caused revolutions in centuries past. Next time a pressure group demands that we spend more public funds on its particular hobbyhorse, remember that it is talking about your money.

Taxes on high earners

A common suggestion to meet the government's need to raise more money is to tax the rich. Sadly, things are a bit more complicated than that. The issue of whether well-off people pay their fair share is difficult and important. It is also one of the most controversial questions in politics today. Can we just tax the rich until their pips squeak? Or would that mean that we all end up worse off than we started? To find out the answer, it is essential we understand more about how tax works and who pays what.

Income tax and national insurance between them (and we've seen they are pretty much the same thing) account for just over half the government's revenue. But who pays all this? The answer, if you have a job or a pension, is that you do. There are 30 million income tax payers in the UK, which equates to roughly half the population. Non-taxpayers include the poor (who we'll come to below), non-working dependents (such as homemakers and students) and 14 million children. As we've seen, retired people pay income tax on their pensions and other income, but not national insurance.

If you are well paid, you pay a lot more tax than the average, as you'd expect. Politicians go on about fairness a lot, but what they are most concerned about is maximising tax revenues while upsetting the fewest number of people. After all, they want us to vote for them. That means all decisions on taxation are a mix of the economic and political.

Do the rich pay their fair share? That depends on what we mean by 'fair'. Let's start with the so-called '1%'. What proportion of the total amount of income tax do you think the top-earning 1% of British taxpayers, that is, the top 0.5% of the British population, currently pay: 10%, 20%? More or less? Bear in mind that these people enjoy over 10% of all taxable income (so they are very well paid).

Having decided that, what figure do you think would be fair?

In fact, the top 0.5% of the British population pay over a quarter of all income tax. That is 10% or so of the government's total tax take. The top 10% of earners pay over half the income tax, which is about £100 billion a year. Just 5% of the population pay more in income tax than the rest of the population put together.

Is that fair? Most people would say yes. After all, they reckon, 5% of the population are rich, aren't they? As it happens, anyone who earns more than £50,000 a year falls into this category. I have yet to meet anyone earning that amount who considers themselves to be rich, although they are reasonably well-off. But look at this from the other side. As far as the government is concerned, the 5% pay for the entire NHS budget (even though many will have private health insurance), or all basic pensions (although they probably have private pensions too). Without them, the country would be bankrupt. Put bluntly, the 5% pay for the public services that they don't really need but that the rest of the population do.

Luckily, the 5% seem reasonably content to carry the load for everyone else. Part of the reason for this is that tax rates are not seen as confiscatory (even if they are, as we have seen, a lot higher than people realise). Any democratic government, whether left or right wing, tries to pile as much of the tax burden as it can onto a small number of rich people. That's just sensible politics. The rich only have one vote each, just like the rest of us. In fact, universal suffrage leads to both higher taxes in general (people are more will-ing to pay taxes to representative governments that they have helped to elect) and higher taxes on the rich. Nonetheless, you might think it makes sense for governments to tax high earners far more than they do. Higher taxes on the wealthiest mean less tax on the rest of us. We would then reward the government that reduced our taxes by out-voting the rich.

Funnily enough, this has already been tried. Back in the 1970s, the top marginal rate of income tax was an eye-watering 98%. It was 83% on earnings. When taxes get that high, they rapidly become counterproductive. Instead of raising more money, penal rates of tax lead to less cash being collected and damage the econ-omy in the process.

Part of the problem was that, back in the 1970s, high earners felt no moral obligation to pay all the tax the law stipulated. Avoidance and outright evasion were rife. But that was only part of the problem. Many of the most talented individuals just left the country. This was the era of the tax exile. And it wasn't just pop stars living in Monte Carlo. Exiles were far more likely to be entrepreneurs moving to America or Australia. When the tax burden is heavy, it drives them out of the country so that the economy as a whole suffers. As a result, the government's revenue falls.

Think about it this way: I need a job done and I ask you to do it for me. I'm willing to give you £100 for an hour of hard work, but you have to pay tax on what you receive. If you were subject to 1970s rates of tax, you might only get £17 of the £100 with the rest going in income tax at 83%. You probably wouldn't think it was worth your while. However, if you were subject to today's top income tax rate of 45%, you would be able to keep £55 and be more willing to do the job. The work hasn't changed and the amount I'm willing to pay hasn't changed either. But tax makes a very significant difference to the amount you receive and thus the chance of the job getting done at all.

This is why economists are concerned about marginal tax rates: these tell us what incentive we have to work a little bit harder. Why work over the weekend for some overtime if the government keeps too much of the extra money? Sir James Mirrlees, who has a Nobel Prize in economics to his name, showed that, from an economic point of view, it is best to keep marginal tax rates low. This is because we tend to decide how hard to work based on how much extra tax we'd have to pay on increases to our salary, rather than the total amount of tax we pay on all of it. If you are a higher rate taxpayer and the basic rate of income tax increases, you'll pay more tax, but only on the income you are already earning. That won't make it less worthwhile for you to do some overtime. Your incentive to work harder or advance your career is unaffected. Nonetheless, high marginal rates of tax on the well paid are popular, even if they are economically perverse.

Both Labour and Conservative governments kept the top rate of income tax unchanged at 40% from 1988 to 2009. Of course, you may recall the increase from 40% to 50% imposed by Labour's Alistair Darling in his 2009 budget. This rate applied to incomes over £150,000 and was controversially cut to 45% in 2012 by the Conservative George Osborne. But, at the same time, Darling also increased the tax rate for people earning between £100,000 and £112,950 to 60%. He did this by abolishing the tax-free personal allowance for incomes over £100,000 per annum. Effectively, because they are losing their personal allowance, the people affected are being taxed at both ends. It means that the marginal rate for someone paid £105,000 a year, when you include employees' and employers' NICs, is over 70%. This hidden tax rise, which even many of the people who pay it seem to be completely unaware of, raises far more money than the 45p rate. That explains why, even though people earning £105,000 pay a higher marginal rate than those earning over £150,000, the government has been in no hurry to give high earners their personal allowances back. Besides, there's been almost no political pressure for it to do so.

The Laffer curve

As we've seen, economists have long realised that when people get to keep less of the money they earn, they work less hard. They stop striving for promotion or a pay rise. They work shorter hours and take longer holidays. In short, high taxes shrink the economy and reduce the tax take. This isn't a question of avoidance or evasion: it's about taking away the incentive to work.

The apparent paradox, that lower tax rates can increase tax revenue, was brought to the public's attention by a US economist called Arthur Laffer in the 1970s. Laffer was having lunch with a couple of US President Gerald Ford's staff at a restaurant in Washington DC. To explain his theory, Laffer drew a curve on a napkin. The idea is simple. If tax rates are zero, the government obviously won't raise any revenue. And if they are 100%, no one gets to keep any of the money they earn, so they won't bother to work. Again, revenue will be nil. This means somewhere between a tax rate of zero and 100%, there is a level that maximises the amount of money that the government can bring in.

Everyone agrees with the theory behind the Laffer curve but, unfortunately, there is no data that tells us exactly what the curve looks like. Economists have tried to construct models using information from various countries, but as the Laffer curve depends on all sorts of variables, the results have not been very illuminating.

When they were advising Alistair Darling in 2009 on how much money he could make raising the UK's top rate of income tax from 40% to 50%, the boffins at HMRC tried to develop a Laffer curve to tell them. However, the result was guesswork and they exaggerated how much tax a 50% rate would raise. Admittedly, Mr Darling was quite happy to be told he'd get more money as this justified the tax rise. When the new Conservative Chancellor George Osborne asked them to review their work in 2012, the boffins revised their Laffer curve to show that cutting the rate to 45% would have a negligible effect on revenues. Luckily, this was what Osborne wanted to hear too. All this fiddling with the rate of income tax should provide more impartial researchers in the future with plenty of data to decide what the Laffer curve really looks like. For the moment, the only way to discover the optimum tax rate is through trial and error.

Governments tend to be pragmatic by nature and will try to tax the rich to raise the most money while doing the least damage to the economy. Nowadays, nobody thinks high tax rates are good for economic growth. It would be an irresponsible politician who seriously argued that he or she should increase tax rates but decrease the amount of money raised just to make things more equitable. So the question is simply: what rate of tax raises the most cash in the long term? Without an accurate Laffer curve, this isn't easy to answer. For a start, it takes several years for all the effects of a tax change to become apparent. It's not so much that people suddenly stop working or move abroad. Gradual effects are more important. People go to the trouble to arrange their affairs in a tax efficient way, whereas before they might not have bothered. The country becomes less attractive to foreign investment and high-earning immigrants who might have considered moving here. And the incentive to better ourselves by working hard to earn promotion and a bigger salary is blunted, to the detriment of the economy as a whole.

Over the last couple of decades, most Western countries have settled on a top rate of income tax of between 35% and 45%. Recent work by the accountancy firm PwC calculated the real marginal rates for someone earning $400,000 for many different countries. For the UK, this came to 43%. In Germany and for an American living in New York it was 40%. So, it's no accident that the Labour government, in office from 1997, maintained the 40% top rate introduced by Conservative Chancellor Nigel Lawson in 1988. It looks like the most sensible number, albeit one subject to an inexact calculation.

Of course, fairness is all-important if any tax system is to enjoy popular consent. If it was just a question of money, we could raise tax rates on ordinary people since there is little that they can do to avoid them. They are already hard pressed, so they have no choice but to work, whatever their marginal tax rate. Fairness is why we have a system where 5% of the population pay half of all income tax. What the Laffer curve tells us is the rate of tax that will bring in the most money. Increase rates beyond that level and revenues fall. But that doesn't mean you have to raise tax rates to the highest possible level for all taxpayers. It is only the better off from whom you want to extract as much as you practically can. Nonetheless, as we've seen, there are limits to how much you can tax them without causing more harm than good.

Sports, prizes and betting

Sometimes you just have to accept that, with tax, fairness takes second place. For example, in the 2012 budget, George Osborne gave some of the world's best-paid professionals a stunning tax break. I'm not talking about the 'tax cut for millionaires' when he reduced the top rate of income tax. True, reducing the 50p rate grabbed all the headlines. But it wasn't just bankers who had reason to be grateful to George. He exempted another group of highly remunerated individuals from UK tax and no one batted an eyelid. That's because the beneficiaries of this generosity were footballers.

Not British footballers like Wayne Rooney and John Terry, but instead Arjen Robben, Thomas Müller and their teammates. They were two of the biggest stars of Bayern Munich who, you may recall, played against Borussia Dortmund in the 2013 Champions League final at Wembley.

Normally, when you work in the UK – even if you actually live abroad – you have to pay tax on the money that you make here. That applies to sports stars as well as visiting business executives. When Tiger Woods or Serena Williams win golf's Open Championships or the tennis at Wimbledon, they have to pay UK tax on their winnings. No one has a problem with that, in part because the tax they pay at home is likely to be reduced by the tax they've had to pay in the UK and other countries where they have competed. But for the biggest stars, the real money is not in the prizes. It is from commercial endorsements and advertising opportunities that result from their high profiles. Serena Williams flashing an Audemars Piguet watch and Tiger Woods wearing his Nike kit are far better remunerated activities than swinging a racket or golf club. Normally, the taxman tries to get his hands on some of this money. This is unpopular with the sportsmen and women, but they are hardly going to forgo the opportunity to take part in premier events like the Open and Wimbledon.

The situation was different when football's Champions League final was played at Wembley in 2013. This is a one-off match where the winner takes all (it's decided on penalties if necessary). Unlike Wimbledon, which always takes place in southwest London, the Champions League final can be played anywhere in Europe. There is no reason for it to be in the UK. One of the conditions that UEFA imposes on the host nation is that it only taxes prize money directly attributable to the game, not any sponsorship and endorsements that the players might have. So, the British government had a choice. Either give all the players tax immunity, or they would take their ball and play somewhere else. When a big one-off sporting event happens in the UK, it is usually because we've promised to relinquish the tax revenue.

Exactly the same exemption from tax was required as a condition for London hosting the Olympics in 2012. In 2013, the Anniversary Games at Crystal Palace took place a year on from the Olympics. Again, the participating athletes had their own special rule in the Finance Act 2013 exempting them from tax, as they did for Glasgow's Commonwealth Games. In the case of athletics, the exemption is designed to persuade just one man to compete in the UK: Usain Bolt. If other countries are willing to give tax incentives to host the big sporting showpieces, we have to match those. It is an example of tax competition, where countries lower their taxes to attract business. Admittedly, there was no special provision for the Rugby World Cup of 2015. Presumably, rugby players don't earn enough to make it worth the lobbying effort.

Sporting stars have often had an easy ride when it comes to taxes. In 1966, England won the football World Cup at Wembley, beating West Germany. The squad, led by Bobby Moore, received a cash bonus for their success. It was the princely sum of £1,000 each. Unsurprisingly, the Inland Revenue took the view that this bonus was part of the players' wages and wanted to subject it to tax. After all, they had earned the money playing football, which was their job. Moore and his players claimed that the bonus was more akin to a prize, which meant that it was not taxable as income. He decided to fight the matter in court. The grateful nation, personified by Judge John Brightman, ruled in Moore's favour so the England team kept their bonuses untaxed.

Nowadays, it's not so simple. If British athletes win a prize or award in the course of their work, HMRC expects them to pay tax on that. A change introduced in 2016 also caps the tax-free proceeds from testimonial matches for retiring professional sportsmen and women. And we'll see in Chapter 5 how HMRC has been fighting a protracted battle with big football clubs over the tax on their players' wages.

These rules also apply to other kinds of award. For example, Hilary Mantel, who is a professional writer, would expect to pay income tax on both of her Booker Prizes, reducing the value of each award from £50,000 to less than £30,000 once it reached her pocket. The rest of us don't have to pay tax on prizes as long as we win them as part of a hobby, whether it is writing or something else. The £5 award for best marmalade at the village show is safe from the taxman as long as the winner isn't a professional producer of citric preserves. However, if he is also selling the preserved fruits of his labours to friends and neighbours, he should pay tax on any profits.

With betting, the tax inspector always wins

Until 2001, betting duty was charged when you put money down at the bookies. In that year, it was abolished by Gordon Brown. You might think this was intended to be a tax cut. It wasn't. The iron law of gambling is that the house always wins. So, instead of taxing the punters directly, the government now charges a levy on the gross profits of the bookies. Of course, the punters still end up paying the tax because the bookies offer less good odds. It is an example of the Second and Third Golden Rules: 'No matter what name is on the bill, all taxes are ultimately suffered by human beings' and 'Taxes are kept as invisible as possible'.

The government also siphons off almost a third of the money from the National Lottery. There is an explicit lottery duty on the revenue from tickets and roughly 40% of the cash for good causes also gets diverted to government projects thanks to some more sleight of hand by Gordon Brown back in 2004. So, not only are the odds of winning the Lottery particularly poor, it is also the most heavily taxed form of gambling.

Other kinds of bet are more tax efficient. You've probably seen the advertisements for spread-betting firms. They claim to provide a tax-free way to speculate on shares on the stock exchange or other financial markets (they also offer more traditional betting markets such as sport and politics). If you invest your savings in shares, you'll have to pay tax on your gains (we'll come to the mechanics of capital gains tax in Chapter 3). So why are spread-betting winnings, which are economically exactly the same as profits from holding shares directly, free from tax?

I once asked this question of the head of tax at one of the City's elite law firms. He admitted that there is no law that states spread-betting gains should be tax free, but nonetheless, as a matter of practice, HMRC doesn't try to tax them. The question was even raised in Parliament in 2013 by a certain Lord Eatwell and the Archbishop of Canterbury. They wanted to know how this tax break could be justified. They thought it was a kind of avoidance and demanded that it cease. The government said the matter was under review and we heard no more.

The government has been wise to kick the matter into the long grass since it knows that spread-betting isn't really tax free. Remember the iron law of gambling: the house always wins. Spread-betting relies on bringing together punters with different views who are willing to wager money on their opinions. A spread-betting firm, like IG Index, acts as the middleman between parties who want to buy and parties who want to sell. IG Index doesn't want to take any risk itself, if it can possibly help it. It makes its money from the spread between the buying and selling prices. As long as IG Index, or at least its computer software, has done its sums right, the winnings of the punters who bet one way will always be less than the losses of the punters who bet the other. The difference is pocketed by the firm.

Well, not all of it. HMRC won't bother to tax the winners because it knows that their winnings will be outweighed by the losses of the losers. In short, the iron law of gambling applies: the house always wins. There isn't much point in taxing anyone apart from the spread-betting firm because it is the only one guaranteed to make money. Effectively, IG Index pays the tax on behalf of all the punters. From an administrative point of view, this is much simpler. And, it keeps betters happy because they imagine that they are hiding their winnings from the tax inspector. In a way, it is a bit like the PAYE system. People betting don't realise that they are being taxed because the spread-betting firm pays it for them.

The poverty trap

Although the better-off pay the lion's share of income taxes, once you factor in the effect of social security benefits, the poor can be hit by very high tax rates. Tax on the low paid is almost as complicated as tax on the rich. It was one of the obsessions of ex-Chancellor and Prime Minister Gordon Brown. He wanted to help the poor, but in the process made the system so convoluted that many people became trapped by it.

Perhaps the most tax-efficient job is being a student working the tables or serving behind the bar. The money you earn, up to £11,000 a year, is tax free because of your personal allowance (although you may be required to pay a bit of national insurance). There is also no tax due on any grant or scholarship that students are lucky enough to win, including gifts from Mum and Dad.

Things are not so rosy for people on benefits, especially lone parents and those in low-paid jobs. They find that tax and benefits interact in a way that exposes them to effective marginal rates of taxation even higher than those with very high earnings. The problem is, when people on welfare benefits move into paid work, their benefits are withdrawn. As they earn a bit more, they find the tax system biting chunks out of their take-home pay as well.

A simple example might explain what the problem is. Imagine that Jane is a lone parent who works part time while her son is at school. It so happens that she now has the opportunity to earn an extra £100 a week by working 10 more hours. For Jane, the effect of an additional £100 a week should be life-changing and perhaps a step out of welfare dependency. However, once all her taxes and benefits are adjusted to take account of her increased income, she finds that she is only £10 a week better off. That means that her effective tax rate is 90%, higher than for someone earning a £100,000 a year. Doing the extra hours is simply not worth her while.

That's the poverty trap: the benefit and tax regimes conspire to deprive the poor of much of the extra money they earn. You'd think it wasn't beyond the wit of man to devise a system that works. Sadly, that's easier said than done. Throughout his tenure as Chancellor, Gordon Brown tinkered with the system to try to make it fairer. But each additional tweak had unexpected consequences that required later adjustments to correct. For example, he wanted to encourage people into work so he provided that the system didn't penalise casual jobs of up to 16 hours a week. Sadly, this just made the transition from casual work to a proper career all the more difficult. Today we have a system of awesome intricacy. The interaction of circumstances, pay, benefits and the number of hours worked is very hard to predict on a large scale. The Tory government has committed to replacing the minefield of interlocking benefits and credits with a single universal credit. The idea is to ensure that no one is exposed to an effective marginal rate of over 63% so they can always take home about a third of what they are paid. That is still too little, and implementing the universal credit itself represents a massive logistical challenge.

There are two ways to deal with the poverty trap. The first is to cut benefits so that the incentives to find a job are much higher. There are obvious problems with this approach, not least that it removes the safety net from those who most need it. Even targeting benefits more carefully takes substantial political will. An alternative approach to the poverty trap would be to pay the same benefits to everyone. Universal benefits, which are not subject to means testing, used to be popular with the political left, but now everyone realises that they are unaffordable. Even child benefit, once paid to all parents, is now denied to families with higher rate taxpayers.

High effective marginal tax rates for the poor, where the government takes back with one hand what it gives with the other, have no moral or economic justification. But this is a problem with no easy answers. Implementing the universal credit and ironing out all its teething problems will take time. Even then, it is still only a partial solution. The poverty trap is still with us.

2

Taxes on what you spend

Value added tax

As everyone knows, value added tax, or VAT, adds 20% to the cost of almost everything we buy, with exceptions including food and children's clothing. Since we buy a lot of stuff, VAT is a very important tax. It raises nearly £115 billion a year in the UK.

VAT was originally structured as a tax on luxuries rather than essentials. This idea has fallen away as the scope of the tax has expanded, most notoriously when domestic heating and power were first made subject to VAT in the early 1990s. The split between luxuries and essentials lives on with regards to food. Most of the groceries we buy from the supermarket are zero rated, but any restaurant meal is treated as a luxury and subject to VAT. Takeaway food is zero rated, but only if it is cold. So, if you visit Pret a Manger for a sandwich to take back to the office, there's no VAT. Eat in, and that's VATable. Get the sandwich toasted, and it becomes subject to VAT whether you stay or go (which is part of the reason sandwich bars charge so much for this service). At McDonald's, because the food is hot, there's always VAT to pay, except when you order a salad or milkshake; unless you consume it *in situ*.

As you can see, this is not straightforward. And I've hardly got going yet.

You may recall a fuss after the 2012 budget over Cornish pasties. VAT is full of little wrinkles, like all other taxes, and one such wrinkle was that freshly baked takeaway Cornish pasties and sausage rolls were not subject to VAT. The reason for this is a little complicated, but revolved around how long you can leave something lying around getting cold before you sell it. Some shops were even claiming that they cooked their food to make it look nice rather than to heat it up.

A Treasury mandarin decided this was incongruous. Hot takeaway food was supposed to be subject to VAT and the situation with pasties was a loophole; in his budget speech, George Osborne briefly mentioned that he intended to close it. What happened next took him by surprise.

The bakers' chain Greggs and *The Sun* newspaper launched a well-orchestrated campaign to force the Chancellor of the Exchequer into a U-turn over the pasty tax. The Labour Party joined in and cunningly characterised the row as Tory toffs taxing the workers' snack of choice (a Cornish pasty) while leaving accountants and lawyers to enjoy their sandwiches tax free. Osborne had little choice but to back down as his budget fell apart. He was already under fire for the cut in income tax for top earners. In other words, politics trumped logic. Under the resulting compromise on pasties, takeaway food remained zero rated if it was cold, or had been heated but was now being left to cool down. Food that is kept hot in a special warming cabinet is fully VATable.

The fiasco was one of the factors that led then Labour leader Ed Miliband to condemn that 2012 budget as an 'omnishambles'. It also shows how difficult it is to reform the tax system. Although there's no logical justification for the VAT treatment of Cornish pasties, trying to iron out this glitch led to howls of outrage from Greggs. They sell a lot of pasties. Not having to charge VAT was a competitive advantage over, say, the neighbouring burger joint. Cue their consternation at any change. The result was that a reform designed to remove a niggle in the way VAT works ended up making the system more convoluted than it was in the first place.

Tax reform nearly always leads to further complications because the losers insist on being compensated and the winners keep quiet. In practice, this means that changing the system is only really possible in an environment of falling taxes when you can minimise the number of losers by ensuring that everyone is better off. If you want to remove a special tax exemption for making widgets, it's easier to abolish the tax in question completely. Extending the scope of the tax to the widget manufacturers is likely to provoke howls of outrage from them and their lobbyists. Before you know it, you'll find that targeting this iconic industry is being portrayed as the fiscal equivalent of drowning kittens. For similar reasons, the attempt to extend VAT to Cornish pasties didn't go well.

Supermarket shelves have been a battlefield over the extent of VAT since it was first introduced. If you look into your trolley while waiting at the checkout, you may find some of the combatants from the great legal struggles over VAT. There was the battle over Jaffa Cakes, compared to which the pasty tax hardly qualifies as a skirmish. Meanwhile, the great Pringle war has gone down as one of the most celebrated court contests in British history. It seems that crisps and cakes lead to fat legal fees as well as increased waistlines.

To understand all the fuss over unhealthy snacks, you need to remember that only basic foodstuffs are supposed to be free of VAT. So you won't be surprised to hear that crisps and sweets are VATable. Biscuits are a special case. A plain old digestive is free from VAT, but if you make them too tasty by coating them with chocolate, then VAT applies. But oddly enough, there is no VAT on cakes. Presumably the draftsman of the law had taken advice from Marie Antoinette, guillotined during the French Revolution. Although the doomed queen had said the common people should eat cake (free from VAT), she had expressed no opinion on Jaffa Cakes. United Biscuits maintained that their product was not a chocolate covered biscuit (VATable) but a chocolate covered cake (no VAT). HM Customs & Excise disagreed.

At the subsequent tribunal case in 1991, lawyers minutely examined the differences between various kinds of baked goods. United Biscuits went as far as to create a giant Jaffa Cake with a diameter of 12 inches to prove that they were cakes. In the end, a determinative factor was how they went stale. The tribunal noted that cakes, like bread, go stiff when stale, while biscuits go soft. A stale Jaffa Cake was produced, tested and found to be hard. Thus, to this day, we can enjoy them without suffering VAT.

The nature of the Jaffa Cake was determined before a special VAT tribunal, a relatively efficient form of justice. The question of whether or not a Pringle is a crisp went all the way to the Court of Appeal in 2009. The law states, uncontroversially, that a crisp is made from fried potato. Distinguishing between crisps and other fried snacks is absurd enough, but the fact a packet of good old British salt and vinegar is subject to VAT at 20%, while tortilla chips are not, adds pecuniary injury to patriotic insult. The situation is hardly better with nuts. A packet of peanuts is subject to VAT, but not a packet of pistachios. However, if you purchase your nuts from the baking ingredients aisle, they are zero rated and hence cheaper.

A lot of money was hanging on the question of whether Pringles were crisps. HMRC wanted Proctor & Gamble to pay an estimated £20 million of extra VAT each year. Two court hearings failed to resolve the question to everyone's satisfaction. Only 42% of the weight of a Pringle is from potato. The rest is mainly corn starch and fat. Eventually, the Court of Appeal was asked to decide: could something be made of spuds if they make up less than half of its content?

Lord Justice Mummery displayed a remarkable amount of common sense in his judgment. Of course Pringles are crisps, he said. Just ask your kids and they will tell you so. The 'question would probably be answered in a more relevant and sensible way by a child consumer of crisps than by a food scientist or a culinary pedant', the Lord Justice of Appeal explained. Expanding on the expertise of his young witness, he went on to remark: 'On another aspect of party food, I think that most children, if asked whether jellies with raspberries in them were "made from" jelly, would have the good sense to say "yes", despite the raspberries.'

The entire dispute must have cost millions in legal fees. It's just a shame no one thought to ask a five-year-old at the outset.

How VAT works

The complexity of the VAT system is a shame because, at heart, the way the tax works is rather elegant. The first point to grasp is that VAT is not a sales tax. A sales tax is added to the price by the retailer and paid directly to the authorities. In the USA, each state and district can set its own sales tax, which means they can vary street by street. Also in the USA, prices are quoted before tax, which only gets added on at the till. This unexpected sting at the cash register makes US sales tax very obvious. Because the tax is so transparent, increasing rates is more difficult than it would be if all prices were inclusive of tax. This is a rare example of a deviation from the Third Golden Rule. Rather than making sure sales tax is as invisible as possible, Americans opt for honesty about the amount people are required to pay.

Here in the UK and the rest of the European Union, all consumer prices have to be quoted gross, that is, including VAT. That means it's another invisible tax we rarely think about paying. Americans are reminded about sales tax every time they buy something. The only time we Britons get the rude shock of seeing VAT added to our bill is when the plumber adds 20% to his very reasonable invoice. You can see the plumber's point. He wants to make clear that he doesn't keep the VAT. He has to pay it over to the government. He's not going to include it in his quotation as if it's something he can control.

So if VAT isn't just a sales tax, how does it work?

VAT stands for 'value added tax' and that is what it is. The tax adds 20% to the value added to goods or services at each stage of their journey from the original supplier to the final user. To really see what is going on, we need an example.

Suppose that Tony the plumber charges you £100 for parts and labour to repair a leaking tap. He adds 20% VAT to the bill, so you pay £120 in total. Let's say the only material he needed to effect the repair was a replacement valve that he bought from Wickes for £40 before VAT. He had to pay 20% VAT on the valve, giving a total cost of £48. Ignoring VAT, you pay Tony £60 more than he paid for the valve. That £60 is the value he added to the valve through his time and skills. In effect, the valve is only worth £40 on its own but is worth £100 once Tony has fitted it to your leaky tap. Since VAT is a tax on the value Tony has added, he should expect to pay the taxman 20% of the £60.

To calculate the VAT Tony owes, take the £20 of VAT you had to pay him and deduct the £8 of VAT that he had to pay Wickes on the valve. That comes to £12 of VAT, which Tony has to pay to HMRC as part of his VAT return. Of course, 20% of the £60 of value added by Tony's labour also comes to £12, so the calculation works both ways.

The same concept works down the chain. Wickes obtained the valve from a wholesaler for £25 plus £5 VAT. Since the valve retailed at £40 plus VAT, Wickes' margin as the retailer and hence the value it adds (by displaying the valve nicely, having assistants to help buyers and ensuring it is available locally) is £15. The VAT that Wickes must pay equals the VAT it charged Tony (£8) minus the VAT charged by the wholesaler (£5), which comes to £3. Alternatively, we could say that the VAT is 20% of the £15 of value added by Wickes, which is also £3.

The wholesaler bought the valve from a factory for £15 plus £3 VAT so pays £2 to the taxman (either 20% of the £10 value added; or the £5 of VAT it charged Wickes minus the £3 of VAT it paid to the factory). The factory purchased copper to make the valve from the foundry for £5 plus £1 VAT (so it also pays £2 to the taxman). The foundry obtained the copper ore from a quarry for 50p plus 10p VAT, so the taxman gets 90p (being £1 less 10p). The quarry pays the last 10p of VAT (see Figure 2.1).

To summarise what's happening here, each link in the chain of suppliers from the copper mine to your leaky tap sees the government paid VAT on the difference between what the suppliers buy and what they sell. That difference between buying and selling prices is the value added at each stage. VAT is a tax on that value

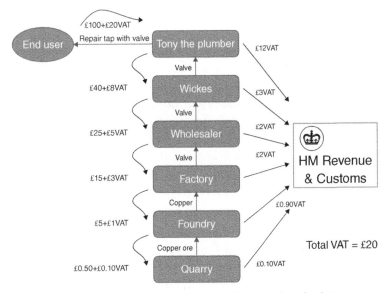

Figure 2.1 How the VAT you pay the plumber finds its way to HMRC.

added, hence value-added tax. Now between them, the miner, the foundry, the manufacturer, the wholesaler, the retailer and Tony the plumber have deposited a total of £20 of VAT into the government's coffers. But remarkably, you suffered all of it when you settled up with Tony and paid him £20 of VAT. Despite the way VAT is paid by people all the way up the chain, the entire cost of it is borne by the end user who effectively reimburses everyone else for the VAT that they have had to pay to HMRC. And because most prices are quoted inclusive of VAT, that end user doesn't even have to think about all the tax he or she is paying.

This makes VAT an excellent example of the Second Golden Rule of tax: 'No matter what name is on the bill, all taxes are ultimately suffered by human beings.' HM Revenue & Customs gets everyone else to do its dirty work and collect the tax up the chain. But, in the end, you and I pay the entire amount.

Zero rated and exempt from VAT

Despite its elegance in theory, the practice of VAT is, as I said before, full of wrinkles. Take the difference between 'zero rated' and 'exempt' from VAT. As we have seen, most kinds of food are zero rated. That means that food is part of the VAT system and a food retailer can reclaim the VAT that they have paid on their costs. However, they only have to add VAT at 0% (which is to say, nothing) to the zero rated food that they sell.

Books are also zero rated in the UK. This is because the government did not want a 'tax on knowledge' when VAT was first introduced. Personally, I've never recognised the pedagogical qualities of novels by Jeffrey Archer or Dan Brown. So really, the zero rating for books is just a tax break for those of us who prefer reading trashy thrillers on the beach to going to the cinema to see the latest Transformers flick (subject to VAT at the full rate) or listening to Ed Sheeran downloads (also subject to VAT).

The printed book market is comparatively small – just £2.8 billion a year. So slapping 20% VAT on books would only raise about £560 million in tax. Simultaneously, it would cause every right-thinking author to crowd the airwaves and newspapers to denounce the government as philistines who want to reduce the great British public to illiteracy. No Chancellor of the Exchequer wants that kind of trouble for a paltry £560 million. So the tax break for books remains.

E-books are subject to VAT at 20% but, until recently, this didn't add much to the price for most of us. When we bought a Kindle eBook from Amazon, the transaction was subject to VAT, but only in Luxembourg where Amazon is based and the VAT rate was 3%. However, from 2015, VAT has to be charged at the rate in the place where the buyer lives, rather than where the seller is. That means UK shoppers now have to pay 20% VAT on e-books. Quite why printed books and electronic ones should be taxed differently is something of a mystery, but the European Court has now ruled that governments are not allowed to levy a reduced rate for e-books.

Then there is the matter of children's clothes and shoes. You probably know that these are zero rated for VAT too. Ladies with small feet have long been able to take advantage of this tax break. They can also avail themselves of the zero rate if they can fit into a smaller bra size (34B, in case you were wondering). Clothes and shoes intended for adults attract VAT no matter how small the size.

Naturally, there are some idiosyncrasies around VAT on children's clothes, not least those to do with goats. Not all goats, by any means: just goats from Mongolia, Yemen or Tibet. This goes back to the essentials/luxuries split. If you are minded to dress your child in a mink coat, that's a luxury so the zero rating for VAT doesn't apply. However, if you merely clothe them in common goatskin, zero rating applies. But, for reasons relating to 1970s fashion that are still reflected in the tax code, the pelts of Mongolian, Yemeni or Tibetan goats are treated as VATable luxurious fur rather than a mere animal skin. If you ever get confused, HMRC provides a handy chart explaining the VAT due on children's clothes made from all sorts of animal pelts including buffalos, gazelles and dogs.

There's no VAT on train, plane and taxi fares because they are zero rated, although you do have to pay air passenger duty on air tickets. This is akin to a sales tax and so it is more straightforward than VAT. The airline adds it to the ticket price and pays it straight over to the taxman. Luckily for families, there is an exemption from air passenger duty for children under 16, which applies no matter what kind of goat skin they are wearing.

As well as the items subject to a rate of zero, there are other things that are 'exempt' from VAT. You don't have to add VAT to the interest you pay to your bank, for instance. Insurance is also exempt, but you do have to pay insurance premium tax when you insure your car, house or holiday, but not your life. The rate of insurance premium tax has doubled since 2015 to 12%, and is likely to reach 20% eventually, so that it is the same as VAT. Also many businesses are not VAT registered because they are not big enough. That means they do not have to charge VAT to their customers.

There is a crucial difference between exemption and zero rating. Banks and insurers don't have to charge VAT on loans and insurance. But neither can they claim it back on the things that they purchase. Effectively, they become the end users who suffer the VAT on the whole supply chain. In a way, they are in the same position as we are when we buy something. We pay VAT on what we purchase and we don't get to charge VAT on things we sell, for instance if we put something on eBay. The VAT that exempt businesses pay on the stuff they buy is called 'irrecoverable VAT'. It costs banks alone £4 billion a year. We're still the ones who end up paying it though. Businesses simply pass the cost on to their customers.

Europe, Brexit and VAT

VAT is intimately tied to our membership of the EU and it is compulsory for all member states to have a minimum standard rate of 15%. The basic rules are decided centrally by the European Commission, which issues directives every member state has to obey. These rules are implemented by national parliaments: in the UK we have the Value Added Tax Act 1994. Individual countries do have a little bit of wriggle room in the scope and rates of VAT, but they can't change anything fundamental. For example, under EU law, VAT rates cannot be reduced below 5%. The only reason that the UK is allowed to have zero VAT on food and books is a special dispensation negotiated when we joined. VAT also helps to determine the level of contributions to the EU. Each member state pays an amount to Brussels calculated from the VAT receipts in that country.

Before the UK joined the Common Market, we had a purchase tax, introduced during the Second World War. This was replaced by VAT in 1973. Purchase tax was a sales tax and was just added to the prices paid by the consumer. VAT was dreamed up in France during the 1950s and is intended to be more broadly based. The system of taxing only the value added at each stage in a supply chain prevents tax being charged twice when the same item is resold. This makes it easier to tax goods and services whether they are supplied to businesses or consumers. The disadvantage of VAT is the complexity that we've already seen. It is also difficult for the UK to reform VAT because all significant decisions have to be made at European level.

One notorious recent example of the inflexibility of the rules on VAT is the tampon tax. As I mentioned, countries in the EU cannot cut the rate of VAT below 5%. This means that the UK is legally obliged to charge 5% VAT on tampons and sanitary towels. Abolishing the tampon tax became a *cause célèbre* with cross-party support that gathered 300,000 signatories on a petition. This put the government in a pickle because it couldn't make any change itself. It promised to take the matter up with Brussels. EU leaders were surprised, at a meeting in March 2016, when the British insisted that they all agree it should be possible to reduce VAT on sanitary products to nil, and that they put out a public statement saying so. Unfortunately, the European Commission has been in no hurry to change the rules, so the only effect of the affair was to demonstrate that we can't even reduce VAT on tampons without Brussels's say-so.

Then came Brexit. On 23 June 2016, the UK voted to leave the EU. Among all the uncertainty this has caused, we can at least be confident that it will lead to a small decrease in the price of sanitary towels, although not until we formally exit. The British government will also be free to make any other changes to VAT that it wishes. However, it is very unlikely we will return to the old purchase tax we had before 1973. Many non-EU countries, from Algeria to Thailand, have adopted VAT in preference to a sales tax, despite the greater simplicity of the latter.

Having similar VAT systems across the EU certainly helps with the smooth running of the single market. However, problems can arise when individual countries fail to implement EU directives correctly. If it turns out that businesses have been paying more tax than they should have been, they can demand a refund, not to mention interest, in some cases going all the way back to when VAT was first introduced. There have been several long-running legal disputes over whether some VAT should never have been payable in the UK and how much the British government has to repay. The worst-case scenario is an estimated £43 billion. It's no surprise that the government is beginning to panic. Last year, it introduced an emergency change to the law to tax the interest on these repayments at a special high rate of 45%, more than twice the normal rate of corporation tax. Whether the full amount will still be payable once the UK leaves the EU remains an open question.

Customs and excise

For most of us, customs officers are the people at airports who occasionally spring into action to waylay an unsuspecting traveller. They work for the UK Border Force, rather than HM Revenue & Customs, and their primary job is to keep track of illegal immigrants and illicit drugs.

The UK Border Force also collects duty on drink and other goods that we want to bring into the country beyond our duty free limits. If you are arriving from elsewhere in the EU, you can bring in as much as you like for personal use. But for travellers from the rest of the world, the threshold is £390 duty free with lower limits for tobacco and alcohol. So, if you bought a top of the range laptop computer while on holiday in the USA, you have to declare it when you come back to the UK. Customs officers charge you the VAT at the same rate you would have paid if you had bought the laptop in the UK. Since looking up the price of a computer is not hard, it is easy to figure out how much tax you have to pay. Fortunately, it is the US price that counts, which, for most computers, is lower than what you would have paid in the high street.

Things get more involved when you have bought a carpet in the Grand Bazaar of Istanbul or a diamond in South Africa. To stop people from using fake invoices to make their items look cheaper than they really are, customs officers are trained to spot high-value goods. More often, though, tourists get ripped off by the merchants.

If the customs officer suppresses a giggle when they see how much you paid for your carpet, the chances are it was not the bargain you hoped it was.

Customs duty is a tax collected on goods when they cross a border. It is among the oldest of taxes, with records going back to the reign of King John in the twelfth century. He reorganised the tariff charged on goods coming into the country in order to raise more money to see off his unruly barons. Raising taxes, or at least ensuring that they were collected, is part of the reason he was such an unpopular king. English monarchs charged customs on the import of certain luxuries, especially wine and later tobacco, sugar and tea. For a long time there were also export duties on goods that the government didn't want to see leave the country, such as wool. English weavers faced competition from Dutch rivals, but since England had the most sheep, a tax on the export of wool made it more expensive for the weavers in the Netherlands to buy raw materials.

Once goods were inside England, there was essentially a free market. Local towns were forbidden to charge tolls or customs so it was cheap to move goods around the country. This contrasted with much of Europe where every town attempted to extort cash from merchants. The Rhine was notorious in this regard. During the thirteenth century, there were twelve tolls on the 120-mile stretch of the Rhine between Cologne and Mainz. Needless to say, this strangled trade.

For the time being, the UK does not control the level of customs duties at its borders, although that is likely to change with Brexit. Customs are currently set by the European Commission and paid over to Brussels. For imports and exports within the European Free Trade Area (basically, the EU plus Norway, Iceland and a few other places) there are no customs duties. The EU also has free trade agreements with various countries, including Switzerland. For the rest of the world, tariffs are charged on imports at various rates ranging from nil all the way up to 85% for goods subject to punitive 'anti-dumping' charges. The system is fiendishly complicated. The full list of tariffs contains over 16,000 different kinds of goods. The rates tend to be highest for agricultural products. For butter and margarine, these are 13% and 16% respectively. For olive oil and sunflower oil, it is over a Euro a litre. Tariffs for cars are also high at 10%. You have to pay these rates whenever you buy a car from Japan or butter from New Zealand. The myriad of different tariffs can easily lead to confusion. A seafood importer was perturbed one day to find that different duty rates applied to the blue grenadier and the hoki, despite the fact these are both names for the same species of fish. In 2016, the Supreme Court was asked to adjudge whether a bra intended for women who had suffered a mastectomy was a fashion item or a prosthetic. Their lordships decided it was the latter and so not liable for customs duty.

Unlike the customs duties imposed by English monarchs, the EU's tariff wall is not primarily intended to raise revenue. It is used to shield certain traditional sectors of the European economy, like agriculture, from global competition. One way that the EU's common agricultural policy keeps food prices high is through adding customs duties to imported food. Tariffs are also bargaining tools to get other countries to agree free trade deals – like the one the EU is currently negotiating with the USA. Free trade means both parties abolish most or all tariffs on goods that they import and export to each other. It is now probable that the EU/USA trade agreement will never come to fruition because of the sheer number of special interests on both sides. In particular, the French insist on special protection for their cultural and agricultural sectors.

Once the UK leaves the EU, it will be able to negotiate its own free trade deals. Overall, tariffs are a relatively small part of the UK tax base so the economic benefits from increased trade as a result of abolishing them would far outweigh the fiscal disadvantages.

Excise duties

While the revenue raised from customs duty is insignificant, excise duties matter a great deal. Excise duties are a tax on things produced or sold in the UK such as whisky and tobacco. And unlike customs duty, they form a large part of the government's income.

Excise, from the Latin for 'cut out', has its origins in the English Civil War when Oliver Cromwell needed to raise money for his New Model Army to defeat the Royalists. After the restoration of the monarchy in 1660, King Charles II was given the proceeds from the excise to cover his personal expenditure. This continued to be how the monarchy was funded until the civil list system was introduced in the late eighteenth century.

All sorts of things were subject to excise at some point. The notorious window tax, introduced in 1696 and levied on the number of windows in a house, was an excise duty. It was brought in because it was easy to count windows from the outside. The earlier hearth tax had provoked outrage because officers of the excise had a right to enter properties to check out the fireplaces. Tax avoidance in those days involved bricking up windows in order to reduce the levy. You can still see blocked frames on many old buildings today, 150 years after the tax was repealed.

The ace of spades is another fossilised relic of the excise. You've probably noticed that in many packs of cards, the ace of spades is decorated with an intricate pattern. Back when packs of cards were subject to excise tax (it was really intended to be a tax on gambling, which was the main thing that cards were used for), the government provided a specially printed ace of spades as proof that the tax had been paid. Excise officers could demand to see the ace when cards were being played. Trying to fake an ace of spades was tax evasion of the grossest sort. Defrauding the revenue in this way was punishable with death by hanging. The excise duty on a pack of cards remained in force until 1960, although the penalties for evasion were a good deal more lenient than in the eighteenth century. Today, only the tradition of having a florid ace of spades remains.

The main excise duties are on drink, tobacco and petrol. Although we grumble about the cost of alcohol, the tax on it is one that many people accept as a price for their sins. The tax is paid at the point of production. When Scotch (or another British-produced spirit) is bottled, tax accrues based on the alcoholic strength of the product. The bottle gets a special label saying UK duty has been paid (much like the ace of spades once demonstrated the same for playing cards). Scotch for export isn't subject to UK duty. It has to be kept in special bonded warehouses while it waits to be shipped abroad. Likewise, UK duty is payable on imported alcoholic drinks before they hit the market.

For a long time the British were not so equanimous about paying tax on alcohol. There was a thriving moonshine industry of illegal booze. The quality was so variable that much of the output was seriously injurious to the drinker's health. In the Scottish highlands, not paying tax to the English king was also a matter of national pride. During the aftermath of Bonnie Prince Charlie's failed rebellion of 1745, the highlands were subject to a brutal regime of land clearances and purges. The whisky distilleries were part of a national resistance, providing the only product that made the hard times bearable. The excise men, who patrolled the mountains searching out the distilleries, did a dangerous job. The most famous of their number was Robbie Burns, now Scotland's national poet, who took the king's shilling as an excise man to make ends meet.

A few years after Burns was collecting taxes, some of the distillers realised that there was a better living to be made selling legal whisky to the English than hiding it from them. George Smith's Glenlivet distillery in Speyside claims to be the first to have gone legit in 1824. The neighbours signalled their disapproval of the move by threatening to burn down Smith's stills. Nonetheless, many other distillers soon followed his example. The British carried the amber nectar of the highlands with them around the Empire and it gained the position it still enjoys as one of the world's pre-eminent spirits. Exports are £4 billion a year and, on top of that, British drinkers contribute another billion in excise duty to the Exchequer.

Today, the tax on spirits is at an all-time high. Buy a bottle of budget whisky, gin or vodka and you are paying about four-fifths of the purchase price directly to the government. Because excise duty is determined by the amount of pure alcohol in the bottle, the tax on a premium whisky is the same as on a cheaper brand of the same strength. However, you have to pay VAT on top of the excise duty.

That means the duty is treated as value added to the product for VAT purposes. Effectively, you pay tax on tax.

There's far more tax per unit of alcohol on whisky and other spirits than there is on beer or wine. The Scotch Whisky Association thinks that this is terribly unfair. But there is logic to taxing spirits more heavily. The theory is to equalise the price of a unit of alcohol in its various forms. At the supermarket, a typical bottle of wine costs about £5 for 10 units of alcohol; a bottle of blended whisky is £14 for 28 units and a large can of beer is £1 for two units. That means, allowing for the cost of the drink and the tax, a unit of alcohol costs about 50p in whatever form you consume it. The reason Scotch is taxed so highly is that, without the duty, it would be unhealthily cheap. It's a good thing when our decisions are not distorted by tax effects and, when deciding how to get plastered, excise duty means that the price of different drinks works out as much the same. Incidentally, this is why a minimum price of alcohol, as suggested by some health charities and politicians, is a red herring. Excise duty has almost the same effect on its own.

Avoiding the tax on alcoholic beverages is very simple. Just don't drink. Travellers also get to avoid duty by buying duty free or bringing cheaper drinks back from Europe. Another possibility is to brew your own. This is much less popular than it used to be, which is a shame as brewing is not difficult and the results can be very drinkable. If you are making your own beer, or a fruit wine such as elderflower or blackberry, it has to be for private consumption only. You shouldn't sell it or even give it away. However, there are special tax breaks for small producers of beer and cider. Cider is usually taxed at the same rate as beer, subject to some wrinkles. But you can make up to 7,000 litres a year, and sell it, without paying a penny of duty. That's over 12,000 pints of scrumpy. While you can't serve it to the public without a liquor licence, you can come to an arrangement with your local pub. The tax break is intended to encourage farmers to preserve small orchards that might otherwise be rooted out. But you don't need to use your own apples and many micro-producers of artisan cider make full use of the tax break and win prizes for the quality of their product. Similarly, since 2002, craft beer can enjoy a reduction in excise duty of up to 50%.

Despite our high duties, there isn't a huge amount of alcohol smuggled into the country today. Most smugglers are concentrating on a far more lucrative trade: tobacco. The ideal contraband is high value and of small size. That means that cigarettes, which are now over £9 for a packet of 20, are ideal. Hand rolled tobacco is, relatively speaking, even more likely to be supplied illegally. The total cost to the Exchequer of tobacco smuggling is estimated to be £2.4 billion a year.

Like the duty on alcohol, the tax on tobacco, at about £7 on a pack of 20, is also extremely easy to avoid. You just have to stop smoking. The government certainly claims that it wants us to do just that. The excise duty on cigarettes is set at a prohibitive rate to encourage us to kick the habit (unlike on alcohol, which, as we saw, is intended to make our tipple of choice the same price per unit of alcohol and maximise revenue). Together with information campaigns and the ban on smoking indoors, this seems to be working. Smokers are now under a fifth of the adult population, down from half 40 years ago. If you are one of the people who find it very hard to give up, the current situation is not pleasant. You either have to pay a fortune to feed your habit, or you could get your fix from the black market. If you are staying honest (and keeping your local tobacconist in business), the rest of us are grateful. The tax on tobacco raises £10 billion a year, considerably more than smokers cost the NHS.

But there is a sting in the tail of this happy story. The fifth of the population who do smoke are drawn disproportionately from the poor and underprivileged. They are the people least able to pay the £10 billion in tobacco taxes that the government collects each year. This means that the duty paid by smokers is one of the most regressive taxes in the UK today. Most people agree that those with the most money should pay the most tax, which is called a progressive tax system. And, as we've seen, this is basically what happens. The top 1% of earners pay over a quarter of all income tax. And the well off also pay more VAT as their expenditure on purchases subject to that tax is higher than for the poor, who spend a higher proportion of their income on food and housing. But the duty on cigarettes is a glaring exception to this rule, which makes it extremely unfair. A smoker on a packet of 20 a day is paying £2,500 in tax on cigarettes every year – a huge amount for someone who is already poor. Perhaps the government could spend more helping people to give up, for example by subsidising e-cigarettes: probably the most effective aid to quit but prohibitively expensive for the less well off.

Still, if everyone stops smoking, the government will have to find another £10 billion to replace the revenue from cigarettes. No prizes for guessing who will have to pay that. Yes, it will be us.

Fuel duty and green taxes

Filling your car up with petrol is one way to pay a lot of tax very quickly. Every time the tumbler turns to show you've added a litre of fuel to your tank, you've paid 58p of duty to the government. That's not quite as high a proportion of tax as for Scotch whisky, but it's close.

The tax on petrol and diesel is another excise duty. Originally, when having a car was a luxury that few could afford, taxing petrol was a good way of extracting extra cash from the wealthy. People with bigger cars had to pay more and the majority without a car didn't pay. This made the tax on petrol reasonably progressive. But as more people acquired cars (there are now 26 million in the UK), not to mention the growing importance of trucks to the freight industry, fuel duty lost any association with fairness. At the same time, the amount it raised increased until it became a central element of the government's income.

The Third Golden Rule of tax tells us that it's easier to impose stealth taxes than taxes that are visible and paid directly. Fuel duty is a classic hidden tax. You don't see it on your till receipt and it is collected from the oil companies, even though it is consumers who pay it. Few people know the rate or the exact amount that they pay each time they fill their tanks. This means it is the perfect stealth tax and, in 1993, was ripe for increase.

There was a further advantage to taxing petrol. In 1989, the Green Party had received 15% of the votes in the European elections. Environmentalism was beginning to become more than just a fad. That meant taxes on pollutants and energy could be presented as good for the planet, providing political cover for unpopular tax rises.

In 1993, with the country sporting a large budget deficit in the aftermath of a recession and the spending splurge that had helped John Major's Tories win the 1992 election, tax rises were essential. Unfortunately, the recession had been made deeper and longer by Major's decision to join the European Exchange Rate Mechanism (from which the UK had been ejected on Black Wednesday – 16 September 1992). Green taxes looked like the way to go.

In his budget of March 1993, Norman Lamont, then the Chancellor of the Exchequer, introduced the fuel duty escalator. He pledged to increase fuel duty by 3% more than the rate of inflation every year. Lamont was sacked a few weeks later, but his successor Kenneth Clarke increased the escalator to 5% over inflation. Gordon Brown went even further in his first budget of 1997 and accelerated the rate of the escalator to 6% over inflation.

The government became adept at blaming the oil companies for increases in the cost of petrol. This was a bit rich given that, by 2000, taxes made up 80% of the price. Petrol at the pump tracks wholesale prices reasonably closely, both up and down. But the public's distrust of big business is almost as great as its suspicion of politicians, so the oil companies received a good deal of flak for price rises caused by fuel duty. But, in the end, even the stealthiest of taxes have to break cover.

Modern Britain's most significant tax revolt, the fuel protests, began on 8 September 2000 when a group calling itself Farmers for Action blockaded an oil refinery in Cheshire. The protests quickly spread to other facilities and the oil companies suspended deliveries. To be honest, blockade is too strong a word for what was happening. There were never enough demonstrators to fully besiege the refineries or even block all the exits. However, no one wanted to play games with a fully loaded petrol tanker, so the trucks stayed in their depots and fuel deliveries to service stations ceased across the country. Fears of fuel shortages triggered panic-buying by motorists. The television pictures showing queues of motorists trying to fill up their cars only encouraged more people to rush out with jerry cans to ensure they had enough fuel. Within a week, many filling stations had run dry. Belatedly realising the potential for crisis, the government took emergency powers and ordered oil companies to recommence deliveries. With public opinion ebbing away, the protesters ended the blockades.

The fuel protestors themselves were astounded by the way their protest rolled up into a national emergency. And while the demonstrations were never repeated with the same vehemence, arguably they never needed to be. The original blockades had been a success. A few months after they ended, Gordon Brown froze fuel duty. Since 2000, the tax on petrol and diesel has generally only gone up by the rate of inflation. The Conservatives, ever sensitive to the needs of motorists, have frozen the duty. The fuel protests showed that there are limits to how far stealth taxes can be increased before people start to complain.

The other main tax on drivers is vehicle excise duty. This is administered by the Driving and Vehicle Licensing Authority (the DVLA) and brings in almost £6 billion a year. Since the duty payable depends on the carbon dioxide emissions of the vehicle in question, it is ostensibly another green tax. We used to indicate that we'd paid it by sticking a tax disc on our car windscreen. The changeover to a fully computerised system in late November 2014 caused no end of confusion for motorists, and teething problems led to the number of untaxed vehicles on the road doubling.

At least classic car enthusiasts don't have to worry about vehicle excise duty. If their pride and joy is over 40 years old, it's exempt from tax and it can even sport old-fashioned black and white number plates to signal that it is of the requisite vintage. More eccentrically, drivers who think a windscreen looks naked without a tax disc can order a facsimile from any year to enhance their cars' period looks.

Oil and gas extraction

As well as charging fuel duty at the pump, the government also collects taxes when oil comes out of the ground. Oil companies are required to pay an especially high rate of tax on the profits they make from extracting oil and gas. This means that North Sea oil and gas producers paid £11 billion in tax in 2011 – even though the rates of production had come down since their peak in 1999. However, the recent slump in oil prices has seen tax revenues fall dramatically to zero in 2016, leaving a large hole in the government's revenues. For the Scottish National Party, which was depending on North Sea oil to finance an independent Scotland, it is an even bigger problem. That said, the taxation of oil extraction is long overdue for a major overhaul as it becomes more difficult to extract the last dregs from under the sea. The government has launched a review of taxation in the North Sea but this doesn't look like it will be radical enough to deal with the fundamental problem of falling reserves and increased extraction costs.

Fluctuations in the oil price, as well as concerns about climate change, have made alternative energy sources more attractive. In the UK, this tends to mean natural gas, which is both extracted from the North Sea and imported as our fuel of choice. It has the advantage of being cheaper than oil and more environmentally friendly. You can extract a third more energy from natural gas for each unit of carbon dioxide emitted than you can from oil. That is much of the reason behind the fact that the USA has been able to reduce the amount of CO_2 it emits over the last ten years. It has switched from oil to shale gas. Luckily, in the UK, we are also sitting on large reserves of shale gas, in addition to the natural gas in the North Sea. (Shale gas and natural gas are chemically identical, both being methane, but are found in different kinds of rocks.)

Shale gas is buried deep in the earth and has to be extracted using a process called hydraulic fracking. This involves pumping water into the gas-laden rocks to break them down and force out the gas. Producing our own gas is obviously miles better than buying it from abroad, especially from such unpleasant regimes as Vladimir Putin's in Russia. So ensuring the UK tax rules for shale gas encourage its production is essential. The government is proposing to use the same system as it does for the North Sea, but with additional tax deductions allowed on setting up frack pads (as the drilling rigs for shale gas are called).

Green taxes

Rises in gas and electricity bills over the last few years have meant the politics of energy are a live issue. So far, politicians have managed to lay most of the blame for high electricity and gas prices at the feet of the 'big six' energy companies. There is only one drawback with this approach – it simply isn't true. Energy companies make healthy profits but their margins are tight at about 4%, similar to supermarkets like Tesco and Sainsbury's. (In comparison, Apple has a margin of nearly 50% on iPads and iPhones.) The problem for the energy companies is that they have to invest in new power stations to keep the lights on. They need profits to support that investment. For years, the government has been procrastinating about new power generation, and we are now reaching crisis point. These issues have been exacerbated by a policy on energy taxes that is best described as inconsistent. As with the fuel duty escalator, the story began in 1993.

We saw earlier that the Conservative government of the early 1990s was running a large budget deficit that needed to be curtailed. The Chancellor of the Exchequer, Norman Lamont, had to raise taxes. The centrepiece of his budget in March 1993 was apply-ing VAT to domestic fuel. At the time, it was zero rated. You will recall that means the energy companies could reclaim VAT they incurred, and didn't have to charge it to their customers. Lamont proposed that it become standard rated (then 17.5%) with the increase coming in two steps. The first stage happened immediately. VAT on domestic fuel rose to 8%. The second stage, to 17.5%, was to take place the following year. By that time, the Labour Party, together with rebel Tories, had mobilised so that the second increase was voted down in Parliament.

The government had presented the taxing of domestic fuel as a green measure designed to make people use energy more efficiently. The opposition rejected this and the shadow Chancellor, Gordon Brown, promised he would cut VAT on domestic fuel to 5%, the lowest rate permitted by the EU, when Labour got into power. He duly did this after Tony Blair's election victory of 1997. The VAT on our gas and electricity bills remains at 5% to this day. In summary, during the 1990s, the Tories wanted to increase green taxes and the Labour Party wanted to cut them.

Then climate change became an increasingly urgent issue. To help deal with it, Tony Blair's government decided to replace the UK's ageing coal-fired power stations with more environmentally friendly ways to generate electricity. Someone had to pay for these and that someone would be us: energy consumers. Again, we heard the argument that increasing taxes on domestic fuel would force down demand. But this time, VAT was deemed too visible. After all, you can see it added at the end of your electricity bill. There was also the inconvenient fact that Labour had forced the Conservatives to abandon their plan to charge VAT at 17.5% and had, instead, cut it.

So increasing VAT on gas and electricity bills was out of the question. Instead, the government started to add various levies to domestic electricity. These levies are not so much stealth taxes as taxes in deep cover with false names and plausible deniability. Many of them don't own up to being taxes at all. There's the Energy Company Obligation, which pays for insulation for people on low incomes; there's the Renewables Obligation, which subsidises expensive wind and solar energy; and there's the Carbon Price Floor. In total, these disguised green taxes add about 13% to electricity bills, with VAT on top of that. In other words, Labour added as much tax to our energy bills in the 2000s as the Tories were going to in the 1990s. They just changed the taxes' names and hid them from view. After 2010, the Coalition government increased these levies still further.

Now, you may say that insulating people's homes and reducing carbon emissions are laudable things to be doing. I'm not going to disagree. But money we are forced to pay to implement government policies are taxes whatever you choose to call them. It is the lack of transparency that concerns me. Energy taxation is the Third Golden Rule in action: 'Make sure taxes are as invisible as possible.' The plethora of additions to our bills also reinforces the First Golden Rule: 'Lots of small taxes together add up to make big tax bills.'

Global warming

Of course, the point of green taxes is to tackle climate change, albeit rather indirectly. And there is little doubt that the carbon dioxide that we are pumping into the atmosphere is causing global temperatures to rise. In short, that means carbon dioxide is a pollutant. So taxes on energy are a way for us to pay compensation for our action of increasing the amount of carbon in the atmosphere. Let's look a bit more closely at how that works.

When someone crashes into your car, it is usually pretty clear whose fault the accident is. And his or her insurers have to pay the cost of repairs. But sometimes it isn't clear who exactly is causing the damage. Traffic jams cause pollution and make us late, but you can't often say one particular person is responsible for the snarl up. Likewise, when lots of people let their dogs foul the common or pavement, it is hard to assign each individual mess to a particular mutt. Economists call these general costs 'externalities' because they are outside normal market transactions. You can't usually deal with them by charging money to the individuals concerned. Either you have to try to use social pressure or fines to change behaviour: so people clean up after their dogs or travel by public transport. Or you can charge everybody through taxation to deal with the externalities we all leave lying around. British traffic jams and dogs become the problem of the British taxpayer.

With carbon dioxide, matters are a little more complicated. Once in the atmosphere, the gas affects the whole planet. However, it still makes sense to pay the compensation for the resulting pollution to governments. To see that this is right, you don't have to believe that they represent the people as a whole or even act in their interests (in much of the world, they definitely don't). Governments are the only institutions with the legitimacy to force us to pay. They can also use the tax system to collect the money. In short, we need a carbon tax.

Once the money has been gathered, many environmentalists would like to see money used to invest in low-carbon energy or other kinds of fuel efficiency. This is what happens with many of the disguised taxes in our fuel bills. But it could be used for other things. In the case of carbon dioxide, there are good arguments for saving or investing the money to mitigate the effects of global warming when they arise. These are all issues for politicians and pressure groups to argue about. Fortunately, as this is a book about tax rather than public spending, we can leave them to it.

The question for now is how big a carbon tax should be. Assuming we agree that CO_2 is a pollutant and that we should pay for our mess through the tax system, any carbon tax should equal the costs that result from the CO_2 we emit. This requires us to calculate the likely costs and benefits of higher temperatures. Estimates for the cost of CO_2 pollution vary but tend to fall within a range of £25 to over £100 per metric tonne of CO_2 emitted. Let's say the cost should be £75 per tonne which is the high-end figure suggested by the US Environmental Protection Agency. On that basis, how much carbon tax should the British be paying? The government publishes the UK's total carbon dioxide emissions per annum and they come to the enormous number of 400 million tonnes a year. That means about 7 tonnes for each and every one of us. On that basis, we should be paying carbon taxes of £500 each: a total for the country of £30 billion annually. Surely a tax on carbon at that level would have people out on the streets. But look a little more closely and a surprising fact emerges. The annual take from fuel duty on petrol and diesel alone comes to £28 billion. Throw in £6 billion of vehicle excise duty, and we are already paying in excess of the entire theoretical carbon tax of £30 billion that should tackle global warming.

You might have suspected that governments have been using greenery as an excuse to put up taxes that they want to increase anyway. You would be dead right. The argument over green taxes is not whether we are paying enough – we are already paying more than that. Rather, it is a question about what the government should be spending that money on.

3

Taxes on what you own

Capital gains tax

On 10 December 1900, after almost six months of rumination, Lord Macnaghten delivered a judgment in the House of Lords that has shaped UK taxation ever since. 'Income tax,' he declared, 'is a tax on income.' While this sounds like a truism, the portentous words of Lord Macnaghten seriously limited the scope of UK taxation. They meant that if you make a profit, which is classified as 'capital' rather than 'income', then it isn't subject to income tax. Sometimes, it is helpful for a judge to state the obvious.

But Lord Macnaghten's judgment did not explain the distinction between capital and income. With so much at stake, it is no surprise that lawyers have spent decades arguing over where the dividing line should fall. We all have a general idea of the different meanings of 'income' and 'capital'. Income is what you earn day by day and capital is long-term investments like houses and shares. But that doesn't go quite far enough. After all, if you own shares, you also receive dividends from them. And if you let out a house, you receive rent. Dividends and rent, as well as interest earned on corporate and government bonds, are all income.

To illustrate the difference between capital and income, the US Supreme Court Justice Mahlon Pitney suggested back in 1920 that we compare capital to a tree and income to the fruit. Growth in the tree, that is, in the underlying value of our shares or our house, is capital. The fruit of the tree, the dividends and rent that we can harvest from our investment, is income. Many judges have a weakness for elaborate metaphors and Justice Pitney must have quaffed his lunchtime bourbon with particular satisfaction on the day he came up with that one.

Simply put, if you have invested in some shares, any increase in value from changes in the share price will be a capital gain, while the dividends you receive each year will be income. That's easy enough. But what if you only own the shares for a few days? Can a quick buck still be a capital gain? That largely depends on whether you are dealing in shares as a business or just occasionally speculating on the stock market.

This distinction used to be particularly important because, before the 1960s, there was no capital gains tax. Income was subject to income tax. Capital gains weren't taxed at all. So, thanks to Lord Macnaghten (and to be fair, the principle existed long before he uttered it), it was worthwhile to make your money as a capital gain rather than as income. You won't be surprised to hear that an entire industry of tax planning grew up around converting income into capital. One example of this became known as 'bond washing'. By the 1950s, there were bowler-hatted gentlemen in the City of London who did little else. There were loads of variants, all of which tried to turn interest or dividends subject to income tax into capital gains that weren't.

These activities increased the pressure to introduce a tax on capital gains. However, from 1951 to 1964, there was a Tory government that had little enthusiasm for hitting its well-heeled supporters with a new tax. Principle mattered as well. Most orthodox economists agree that taxing capital is not a good idea. It discourages investment and reduces the incentives for entrepreneurs. But something had to be done to protect the income tax base from schemes that converted income into capital gains.

To start with, the Tories brought out a very complicated piece of anti-avoidance legislation called the 'transactions in securities' rules. They were specifically designed to put a stop to aggressive kinds of bond washing and very largely succeeded. A series of court cases in the 1960s and 1970s showed that these rules really had teeth. The transactions in securities provisions still exist, although they now rarely apply. In fact, for young tax trainees who don't know their history, they make very little sense.

But the Labour Party said this didn't go far enough. After they won the 1964 general election, Harold Wilson's Labour government finally introduced capital gains tax. From then on, capital profits have been taxable as well as income. Today, capital gains tax is paid at a rate lower than the equivalent rate of income tax. This means that wealthy people still prefer capital to income. The reason for keeping the rate of capital gains tax low is to encourage entrepreneurs to build up businesses rather than quickly cash in.

One of the main beneficiaries of the low rate of capital gains tax is the private equity industry. Nicholas Ferguson of SVG, a major player in the world of private equity, noted that his fellow tycoons were subject to a lower rate of tax than their cleaners. Which was true. Cleaners pay income tax and NICs on their wages for keeping the moguls' palatial kitchens and bathrooms salubrious. But as much of the profit of private equity funds was treated as capital, Nicholas Ferguson and his colleagues only paid capital gains tax on their share of those profits, not income tax or national insurance.

You may have heard that private equity is a bad thing, running companies into the ground and firing people left, right and centre. However, while some private equity firms are certainly at the more carnivorous end of global capitalism, they are also a good way to inject new money into businesses. Private equity funds often invest in companies that are not doing as well as they should and try to turn them around. If they succeed, they can sell them on at a profit. If they fail, they lose their money. Ensuring that people are willing to risk their shirts in chancy investments is an essential element of capitalism. If the government wants to encourage investment by entrepreneurs, it is reasonable enough that they get taxed at a reduced rate. However, if investors are earning fees or interest, those should be subject to income tax. Only growth in the underlying investment is supposed to enjoy capital gains tax rates.

Nonetheless, fund managers often structured their returns as capital in order to take advantage of the lower rates on capital gains, if their returns were taxed at all. In response, the government has been tightening up the rules to ensure that reduced rates only apply to genuine capital growth, where there could just as well have been a loss if the business had not gone to plan.

UK companies have an almost complete exemption from tax on capital gains they make from selling substantial shareholdings in other companies. All they need to do is hold the shares for a year and ensure the company they are selling is engaged in a proper trading business. The aim is to ensure that tax doesn't get in the way of business investment and is another example of how the government recognises that taxing capital can be damaging economically.

Paying capital gains tax

If you are a typical taxpayer, the chances are you've never paid a penny of capital gains tax. As I mentioned, its main point is to 'bookend' income tax to ensure that people don't pretend their income is really capital. It also catches big gains, such as if you pick up a long-lost painting by Vermeer at a car boot sale and it fetches £100 million at auction. If you enjoy that kind of windfall, the government wants a cut. But most of us aren't in either situation. We can't convert our salary from income to capital and we don't have the eye to spot bargain antiques. So capital gains tax is deliberately designed so it doesn't provide a reason for many of us to trouble the taxman.

For a start, we all have an £11,100 a year tax-free capital gains allowance. That means that we can enjoy substantial capital windfalls without having to pay tax on them. There are also other exemptions so that entrepreneurs don't get hit by a massive tax bill when they sell up or retire.

In any case, the two biggest assets that any of us are likely to own are our house and our car. There's no capital gains tax on either of them. Cars are simply exempt. This isn't the government being generous. Few people get to sell a vehicle for more than they bought it. Most of the time, our shiny new cars have depreciated precipitously into old bangers by the time we dispose of them. That means that we make a hefty capital loss almost every time we sell a car.

When you make a capital loss, such as when you sell shares for less than you bought them, you can save it up to set against any future capital gains you might make from the auction of that fortuitously discovered Vermeer. If all the losses that people made selling their old cars were allowed as deductions from future gains, almost no one would ever pay capital gains tax. So it is better to simply exclude cars from the net altogether. That means no taxable gains, but no losses either.

As a result, classic cars are a tax-free investment. If you bought a pristine Ferrari 250 GTO a few years ago, you might now be able to sell it for £30 million plus. Any profits should not be subject to tax. On a rather more modest scale, I have an old Mercedes in the garage that I enjoy driving around on sunny weekends. I might be able to sell it for more than I bought it (which wasn't much) in a few years' time. Again, there would be no capital gains tax on the profit. However, there is a catch. If you buy an old car with the *intention* of doing it up to sell on at a profit, that profit is taxable. In fact, you would pay income tax on it rather than capital gains tax. That's because you bought the car to make money by doing the work to improve it, not just to let it increase in value on its own. In tax language, a one-off project to make money goes by the delightful title of 'an adventure in the nature of a trade'. I probably won't have to pay income tax on any gains from my Mercedes. I didn't buy it for any other reason except that I enjoy cruising around with the roof down while my children sit in the back complaining about the draught.

Taxes on homes and property

House prices increase because, in the long term, the demand for homes continues to outstrip supply. The population of the UK is growing while the housing stock is going up at a slower rate. Planning laws, not to mention local objections to new developments, mean that this situation is unlikely to change any time soon.

Houses and flats are subject to capital gains tax, like all kinds of real property. But there is a special exemption for our main residences. The exemption is very generous, not least because the gains that it can shelter might be very large. You can even temporarily rent out your house while you move away and still enjoy the exemption. The rules are complicated, so you'll need an accountant to sort them out for you. But to give you an idea of how it works (noting again you should not do anything on the strength of what you read in this book), I rented out my London flat for three years while I took a career break to go back to university. I still didn't have to pay any capital gains tax when I eventually sold it. The biggest restriction on the exemption is that you can only have one main residence at a time. Even so, if you are lucky enough to have multiple houses, you get a lot of leeway on deciding which one is your main residence when you come to sell.

Several high-profile cases have illustrated the flexibility of the main residence exemption. In 2009, the *Daily Telegraph* revealed the expense claims of Members of Parliament. It transpired that some MPs had been claiming Parliamentary allowances for 'second homes'. This is allowed because the constituencies of many MPs are a long way from Westminster, so they need somewhere to stay in London. But when they came to sell them, it turned out these houses were not secondary after all. MPs were classifying them as their main residences, thus exempting them from capital gains tax. One example was the Conservative MP Eleanor Laing. She sold her London flat, which was her second home for the purposes of Parliamentary expenses, for £1.8 million in 2008. By electing to make the flat her main residence for tax purposes, she saved an estimated £180,000 in capital gains tax.

You might think that can't be how the rule is supposed to work. You would be wrong. When a judge is trying to figure out how a particular tax rule should be applied, she'll try to figure out the intentions of Parliament when it passed the law. So the question we should ask Eleanor Laing is, 'Did Parliament intend that you should be able to designate your second home as your main residence to maximise your capital gains tax saving?' In this case, with so many MPs taking advantage of the wheeze themselves, the intention of Parliament can hardly be in doubt. And just to make the point clear, in October 2013, Eleanor Laing was elected by MPs to be Deputy Speaker. They would hardly do that if they thought she was abusing the main residence exemption.

In the end, the government's policy is that people are not expected to pay capital gains tax on their homes. The people who benefit most are older and retired people downsizing after the children have moved out. They can sell a big house, buy somewhere smaller and pocket the difference tax free as a nice little nest egg. Like it or not, that's the way the rules are supposed to work.

However, the government taxes homes in other ways. There's stamp duty on buying a house, council tax while you live in it and inheritance tax when you pass it on to your successors.

Inheritance tax

Houses make up the bulk of the wealth most people have when they die. Inheritance tax is due at 40% of the value of an estate over £325,000. With house prices moving inexorably upwards, more and more estates are being pulled over the threshold. Still, this is another tax most of us never pay (and not just because we're dead by the time the bill becomes due). Of about a quarter of a million estates that HMRC hears about each year, only about 20,000 pay any inheritance tax and it raises just £4.5 billion. Still, wealthy people do spend a lot of time planning how to minimise it. The simplest method is not to die. If you give something away and then resolutely refuse to pop your clogs for seven years afterwards, the lifetime gift ceases to be subject to inheritance tax. You can also bequeath as much as you like to your spouse without incurring any tax. Best of all, you inherit your spouse's £325,000 tax-free allowance, provided he or she hasn't used it up making bequests to people other than you. That means, when you finally pass your estate on to your heirs, the total tax-free allowance might be up to £650,000. Finally, if you give at least 10% of your estate to charity, the tax rate on the rest is reduced to 36%. Of course, the best way to pay no inheritance tax is to spend all your money before you kick the bucket. It is much more fun that way.

The tax was first brought in by William Pitt in 1796 to help fund the Napoleonic Wars. By the late nineteenth century, it was called death duty: a name that could only increase its unpopularity. In 1894, it became estate duty, then capital transfer tax in 1975. It was only rebranded as inheritance tax in 1986 by Nigel Lawson. Among the middle classes who stand to inherit substantial amounts of money from the value of their parents' homes, inheritance tax is obviously very unpopular. When George Osborne, then in opposition, promised to raise the threshold to £1 million in 2007, he spooked Prime Minister Gordon Brown so much he ducked out of calling an early general election.

Osborne did eventually increase the inheritance tax threshold to £1 million, although the increased limit only applies when you are passing the family home on to your children and the total estate of you and your spouse is less than £2 million. The full increase in the threshold doesn't even come into effect until 2020.

Speaking personally, I have always considered inheritance tax to be one of the fairest of taxes. No one deserves to inherit a fortune just because they have wealthy parents and it's right that some of the largesse must be paid away as inheritance tax. However, it could be better designed. For example, avoiding inheritance tax on a gift if you live for another seven years relies on sheer good fortune. It's also complicated: the government's office of tax simplification counted 91 reliefs from inheritance tax. A better tax would be imposed at a flat rate of, say 20%, but with many of the exemptions abolished.

The exemption for bequeathing a business is particularly gener-ous, allowing qualifying businesses to escape inheritance tax com-pletely. But as well as costing the government a lot of money, business property relief also means that businesses are not as well run as they could be. If Dad made a fortune from widget-making, it doesn't follow that his children are best placed to carry on the trade. It might be better managed by someone outside the family with acu-men for widgets. Unfortunately, the tax system encourages an entre-preneur's children to continue managing his business rather than doing what they are good at themselves. In fact, research by econo-mist John Van Reenen has suggested that family businesses, after the first generation, are less well managed than businesses run by their founder or someone completely unrelated.

Stamp duty land tax

Stamp duty is one of the oldest taxes still in existence. The idea originally came from the Netherlands and was imported into Great Britain when the Dutch *stadtholder* William of Orange became King of England in 1688. Various official documents, such as insur-ance policies, had to be written on special stamped paper to be valid. Stamp duty was the charge people had to pay the government for the special paper. It was intended to be a short-term expedient to finance King William's war with France, but instead it has been retained ever since. An attempt to extend stamp duty to the British colonies in the eighteenth century was not an unqualified success. American colonists rioted when the stamped paper was imported to the New World, most famously in Boston in 1765. Although the Stamp Act was soon repealed, the resentment it had caused helped to spark off the American War of Independence. However, even the loss of America failed to halt the forward march of stamp duty.

It was not until 1808 that the scope of stamp duty expanded to include buying and selling land (technically known as conveyance). The current incarnation of stamp duty on property was introduced by Gordon Brown in 2003 and is called stamp duty land tax. It is simply a surtax on the purchase price of property when it is bought and sold. To register the title of some land you had just bought, you used to have to take the deeds to be stamped by a government official. You were then recognised as the legal owner of the property in question. If you didn't bother to pay the stamp duty, you would not be able to assert in the court that you were the true owner of the land. Among other things, that meant you had no legal right to receive rent or evict squatters. Although you no longer need to get anything physically stamped, you still have to pay the required stamp duty land tax before the Land Registry will register your property.

In the 1990s, stamp duty was just 1% and applied only to what were, back then, relatively expensive properties of £60,000 or over. But from 1997, Gordon Brown started to increase the duty as he realised that the booming housing market meant that there was lots of money to be collected from it. In 2003, he modernised the system and relaunched stamp duty on property as stamp duty land tax. He also kept bumping the rate. Now stamp duty land tax can reach 12% for the most expensive homes and it brings in over £10 billion a year.

There's no stamp duty on homes sold for up to £125,000. For more expensive residential property, the rates escalate and, until December 2014, you had to pay the stipulated percentage on the entire cost. For example, the stamp duty on homes worth between £125,000 and £250,000 was 1%. But as soon as the cost went above £250,000, the stamp duty rate rose to 3%. That meant stamp duty on a £250,000 flat was £2,500 (1% of £250,000), but if the price of the flat increased by one pound to £250,001, the stamp duty tripled to £7,500 (3% of £250,001). This sudden jump in duty was unfair and distorted prices. So in his Autumn Statement of 2014, George Osborne reformed the system. Today, there is still no stamp duty on homes up to £125,000. However, for more expensive properties, it is charged at 2% of the price over £125,000, then 5% of the price over £250,000, all the way up to 12% of the price over £1,500,000. The result of Osborne's reform is that stamp duty now increases more smoothly, while the overall rates on the most expensive properties almost doubled.

The high rates of stamp duty for luxury houses have encouraged people to avoid the charge if they can. A simple way for them to do this is to hold their homes in a company registered abroad. The BBC's foreign correspondent John Simpson did this, keeping his London house in a Bahamas registered company. If he wanted to sell the house (which would attract stamp duty land tax), he'd just sell the company instead. The scheme could also save inheritance tax from being paid on the house if the owner of the company isn't domiciled in the UK. John Simpson got cold feet and exited the arrangement in 2012, but it still often made sense to hold property in a company, especially for those people based outside the UK. The government has now enacted a new tax specifically to discourage holding houses through companies. This is intended to make sure that foreign buyers of London property have to pay the same tax on buying or selling them as the rest of us.

Judging by the expense of a plush des res in Kensington or Mayfair, not to mention house prices in many other parts of the capital, it looks like neither Brexit nor the increases in stamp duty over the last few years have dampened demand. Nonetheless, stamp duty may be damaging from an economic point of view. The TaxPayers Alliance (TPA) has described it as 'one of Britain's most iniquitous and arbitrary taxes'. Admittedly, the TPA is an outfit that has never met a tax it likes. However, there is evidence that high transaction costs make markets less efficient. The practical effect of transaction costs like stamp duty and legal fees is to increase the chance of booms and busts. When it costs money to buy and sell homes, people are less likely to enter the market when prices are falling. This means that the supply of housing dries up, pulling prices down even further. In a boom, high transaction costs can have the opposite effect because people pile into a rising market thinking they can make a profit to cover the cost of a sale.

Economists also recognise that the costs of moving house, like stamp duty, are among the factors that increase regional unemployment because they make it harder for workers, especially those with families, to move to where the jobs are. Admittedly, most of these costs only apply when buying a house, not when renting. The high cost of housing in the UK is a much bigger problem. As I mentioned earlier, the main force driving up house prices in the UK is the fact that there are not enough of them. Strict planning laws and local objections mean that the construction of new houses is difficult and expensive. It's no surprise that the ones that do get built are often costly.

Stamp duty is now very hard to avoid if you want to buy a house, brings in much-needed billions and hasn't caused social unrest. This means that we can probably expect rates to increase further. After all, the main argument against taxes on purchases is that they depress activity in the market. If the London housing market can take stamp duty at 12% in its stride, the government may be tempted to see how much more the market will bear.

Council tax

Stamp duty land tax arises when houses are bought and sold. There's logic to this. The government only wants to receive cold hard cash, so the best time to levy a tax is when money is passing from one person to another. That's why we suffer income tax and national insurance when we are paid, VAT when we go shopping, and stamp duty on buying a home.

Council tax isn't like that, which is one of the main problems with it. We have to pay it from money we have already received. That means it contravenes the Third Golden Rule: taxes are kept as invisible as possible. Council tax wears a hi-vis jacket and it is resented accordingly. It raises £24 billion a year, which is shared between local authorities and the emergency services. The actual amount you have to pay depends on where you live, since counties, boroughs and even parishes can all set their own rates.

The amount of council tax we pay is related to how much our homes are worth. There is a 25% discount for homes with only one adult, and a 50% discount for houses full of students. Empty properties may have to pay more or less depending on how long they have been vacant.

Each home is assigned to one of eight bands, A to H, based on its market value on 1 April 1991, before council tax was first introduced as a replacement for the poll tax. That means a house that was worth £320,000 in 1991, so in the top band H, is likely to cost £1.2 million today. Despite the valuations being a quarter of a century out-of-date, no government wants to grasp the nettle of a major revaluation. If it ever happens, there will be winners (who'll be quietly satisfied) and losers (who'll scream blue murder). For example, factors like 'gentrification' would mean less wealthy people who own houses in up-and-coming areas would find their bills increasing.

Nonetheless, if you think your own house is in the wrong band, you can ask for a re-assessment by the valuation office agency. Beware though: it is possible that your home will be re-valued upwards so you end up paying more. In 2015, one resident in a terrace of identical houses in Lynton Avenue, Hull, complained it was unfair that her home was in a higher band than her neighbours' were. The valuation office agency agreed and increased the banding for all the other houses in the street, while leaving the original complainant's unchanged.

Buy to let

It's difficult to believe that 20 years ago private landlords hardly existed. Until the late 1980s, the rental market was stymied by the fact that once a tenant had moved in it was almost impossible to make them leave. And if you wanted to get a mortgage to buy a flat to rent out, you'd find banks and building societies were unenthusiastic. The first issue was dealt with by the Housing Act 1988 which introduced assured shorthold tenancies that allow landlords to ask tenants to vacate the property after an agreed period. Then, in September 1996, the Association of Residential Letting Agents teamed up with four lenders to launch the buy-to-let mortgage. The era of the private landlord had begun.

The buy-to-let boom has had undoubted positive effects. Lots of new capital has been injected into the UK housing sector, with landlords doing up derelict flats and massively increasing the supply of rented accommodation. At the same time, buy-to-rent is blamed for driving up house prices and making it more difficult for people to purchase their own homes, especially in hot spots like London and the university towns.

Buying to let also used to be quite tax efficient. Landlords have to pay tax on the rent they receive from tenants. However, they can deduct their buy-to-let mortgage interest from the rent when they calculate their taxable income. That's because, unlike mortgage interest on your own home, buy-to-let mortgage interest is treated as a tax-deductible expense. Where they included furniture, landlords could also automatically reduce their taxable rental income by 10% because of a flat rate 'wear and tear' allowance, regardless of whether they were really spending 10% of the rent on repairs and maintenance.

The way landlords can deduct mortgage interest from their income means that they can take advantage of a concept called 'leverage'. This allows them to supercharge their investment return and works as follows. If I buy a house and it goes up in value, I get to enjoy all the increase. Even if it is subject to capital gains tax, we've already seen that the relevant tax rate is lower than on income. Say I bought the house with a mortgage, putting down a 25% deposit. That means I can buy a house four times more expensive than I could afford without the mortgage. However, I still get to keep 100% of any increase in the value of the house, quadrupling my gain. As long as the rent I am receiving from my tenant is enough to cover the interest on the mortgage, I am effectively enjoying any increase in the value of the house for free. Thanks to leverage, the returns from buy-to-let have been higher over the last 20 years than almost any other kind of investment. As long as house prices kept rising, buy-to-let landlords kept on raking it in.

Then, in 2015, the party stopped. George Osborne decided it was time for the private rented sector to pay a bit more tax. He introduced a 3% surcharge on the stamp duty land tax due when buying a second home or buying to let. And, for good measure, he scrapped the 10% blanket 'wear and tear' deduction from taxable rental income. But the biggest change was how he reduced the benefits of leverage. Mr Osborne announced he would be restricting the tax relief for mortgage interest to the basic rate of income tax, diverting a huge chunk of the returns from buy-to-let into the welcoming arms of the taxman. Previously, landlords could deduct all the mortgage interest they paid from the rent they received, only suffering tax on the net amount. The change means that many will effectively only be able to deduct half their interest payments from their rent receipts when calculating tax bills.

It isn't yet clear what the long-term effects of these reforms will be. No doubt, if buy-to-let continues to enjoy rude health, the current Chancellor of the Exchequer, Philip Hammond, will find some way to tax it even more.

The mansion tax and wealth taxes

Labour and the Liberal Democrats went into the 2015 election promising to introduce a mansion tax where people would pay an annual levy based on the value of their homes. Both political parties suggested anyone living in a house worth £2 million or more would have to pay £2,000 or £3,000 each year. They expected the tax to raise £1 billion.

The mansion tax is a kind of wealth tax, meaning a tax on what we own rather than what we earn or spend. A typical wealth tax requires you to add up the value of everything you own, including your house and any investments. You then have to pay a percentage of your total wealth over a certain threshold each year. For example, you might have to pay 1% of your wealth over £1 million. So, someone with a house worth £5 million and investments worth £2 million would pay £60,000 per annum.

Wealth taxes are currently getting plenty of attention. In 2016, the Labour Party explicitly proposed to introduce a tax on all wealth instead of just on mansions. The celebrity economist Thomas Piketty has suggested that they are the best way to cut inequality and raise government revenue. You can see why. The total wealth of the UK population is estimated to be well in excess of £10 trillion, and almost half of that wealth is in the hands of the 10% of households who each have assets of at least £1 million. If we taxed those millionaires 1% of their wealth a year, we would raise a whopping £50 billion. But when we get into the nitty-gritty, things become more difficult: £2 trillion of the wealth we are trying to tax is in pension funds, which it would be politically impossible to touch. Of the rest, we would need various exemptions for older people who own an expensive house but don't have much income to pay a hefty new tax. In fact, any tax that is concentrated on the old is likely to be a vote loser. Pensioners are renowned for being more willing than other groups to get to the polling station and, as a result, governments try not to antagonise them.

Back in the 1970s, the Labour government committed to introducing a wealth tax, but after several years of effort gave up. It turned out to be impossible to frame a tax that would raise enough money to make the political fallout worthwhile. Many countries that have implemented wealth taxes – including Denmark, Germany and Sweden – have since got rid of them. France still has one, but it is controversial and many economists want to abolish it.

To understand the main political problem with wealth taxes, ask yourself if you enjoy paying your council tax bill. I doubt it. People with bigger houses pay more but the tax is still extremely unpopular. The money sails out of our current account every month. For those affected, a wealth tax would be much worse. For example, a doctor living in London earning £120,000 a year who bought her family house ten years ago could very easily find it is now worth over £2 million. That doctor would have to pay thousands in additional tax a year from money in the bank on which she has already suffered income tax and national insurance at an effective marginal rate of 67%. The situation for a pensioner with an expensive house but low income would be intolerable. They would probably have to sell up just to the pay the tax.

This means that a mansion tax or a wealth tax is superficially attractive, but more difficult to implement in practice. It is unlikely one will be introduced in the UK.

Taxes on pensions and saving

We are always being encouraged to embrace thrift and save regularly. The government is especially keen that we should put money aside for our retirement.

Saving for retirement is definitely a good idea. You'll recall we looked at the basic state pension in Chapter 1. Everyone who pays national insurance gets one but, as we saw, it isn't worth very much. Many of us have other pension schemes that run in parallel to the state pension. If you work in the public sector, you are likely to have a final salary scheme. You pay into this each month and, when you retire, you receive a pension that is a fixed proportion of your final salary. This is one of the biggest perks of working for the government since, unlike the state pension that you 'buy' with national insurance contributions, these final salary schemes are very good value for the beneficiary. Unfortunately for the rest of us, our taxes are making up the difference between the true cost of these schemes and the amounts that public sector workers have to contribute to them. Because the government's future liabilities to pay retirees who have public sector pensions is 'off the books' the true scale of the national debt is much greater than the official figures. Some estimates of the total amount the government will eventually have to pay out for underfunded public sector pensions exceed a trillion pounds, which almost doubles the total national debt of the UK.

And that money must come from our taxes, just like all other government expenditure.

There are a few final salary schemes in the private sector as well, but they are becoming increasingly rare. With final salary schemes, you pay contributions into the pot, but that might not be enough to pay the agreed pension when you retire. Where the pension scheme is in deficit (meaning it doesn't have enough money to pay for all the pensions it is supposed to), employers have to top it up to ensure that when their staff retire, the money is there to pay the pensions. For large companies, the bill can come to billions of pounds. Conversely, in good times, if the pension fund is full to overflowing, the company might be able to cut back on the contributions it makes. The result is extra profits in good times but vast extra costs when the economy is in the doldrums and businesses desperately need to make savings.

Because of the problems funding final salary schemes, most of us now have a pension scheme where we pay in an amount each month and get a pension from whatever is in the kitty when we retire. These are called money purchase or defined contribution schemes. It is worth talking about them in a bit more detail because the way they function is tied very closely to their tax treatment.

In brief, the system works as follows: you pay in as much or as little as you like each month (and your employer sometimes pays in something as well). This amount is tax free, so you don't pay income tax on the part of your earnings that you pay into your pension fund. To see what that means, remember the marginal tax rate that we discussed in Chapter 1. Suppose your marginal income tax rate is the basic rate of 20%. Ignoring national insurance, that means that for each £100 increase in your salary, you only take home £80. However, if you paid that extra salary into your pension fund instead, you'd get the full £100 of credit. You have to pay national insurance on the money you pay into your pension, although there is a government-approved kind of tax planning called 'salary sacrifice' that saves you the national insurance too.

You can contribute £40,000 to your pension tax free each year, and there is a limit on the total pension savings you can build up. The money is invested by the pension fund manager but you often get some say on what it is invested in. The income and capital gains from these investments are added to your pension pot, again tax free. So the pension pot suffers no direct tax while it is growing.

That sounds great. We can pay money into our pension schemes without being taxed, and then the money we've saved grows tax free as well. However, pension funds do still suffer tax indirectly when they receive dividends from companies. We'll talk about corporation tax in more detail in the next chapter. But for the moment it is worth remembering that a fair bit of your pension fund will be invested in blue chip shares in companies like Vodafone and BP. If you have a pension, you are a part owner of these companies and so any tax they suffer is really suffered by you. That's because when a pension fund receives a dividend on a share, that amount represents profits of the company after it has paid corporation tax. That company taxes end up being paid by real people is a prime example of the Second Golden Rule of tax: 'No matter what name is on the bill, all taxes are ultimately suffered by human beings.'

The position is the same, incidentally, if you receive dividends on shares you hold in an ISA. Even though you may not pay any direct tax on the dividend, you do suffer the underlying corporation tax. If you hold shares directly, you pay income tax on the dividend, even though it has been paid out of company profits that have already been taxed. However, in this case, the rate of income tax is reduced to reflect the corporation tax already paid.

It wasn't always like this. In his first budget in 1997, Gordon Brown abolished the repayment that pension funds used to receive to compensate them for the corporation tax that companies had paid on their dividends. This was the 'great pensions raid' that you may have heard of. By some estimates, this has cost pension funds £118 billion over the last couple of decades. To be fair to Gordon

Brown, the old system of only giving tax credits for dividends from UK companies was probably illegal under EU law. And, at the same time, Brown radically simplified the corporate tax system, getting rid of a tax on dividends called 'advance corporation tax'.

A more recent change was the 'pensions freedom' that George Osborne announced in his budget in 2014. Under the old rules, when you retired, you had to use most of your pension pot to buy an annuity from a life insurance company. An annuity is a promise by the life insurer to pay you an agreed income for the rest of your life in exchange for you paying them a lump sum when you retire. Annuity rates have been notoriously poor in recent years, thanks to low interest rates and the fact we are living a lot longer after retiring. Unfortunately, the income from an annuity is also taxable. The tax advantages of saving for a pension disappear after retirement, and income tax (although not national insurance contributions) is chargeable on annuity payments you receive. You are also allowed to take a tax-free lump sum on retirement, but the amount is limited to 25% of your pension pot.

'Pension freedom' changed these rules. On retirement, you are now able to take the money out of your pension pot and do what you want with it. The downside is that when you take the money out, you have to pay income tax on the withdrawal at your marginal rate, meaning the rate of income tax you pay on your highest slice of income. You still get a 25% tax-free lump sum. If, instead, you buy an annuity (which you are still allowed to do), you only pay tax when you receive the annuity payments down the line. So freeing up your pension fund can land you with a big tax bill upfront. That's why the government calculates that pension freedom will increase tax yields in the short term.

With pensions, you get great tax advantages when you pay in, but you get taxed when you retire. Effectively, tax is deferred at the time you originally earn your income, but you still have to pay it at the time you finally receive the money as a pension.

Other ways to save

There are other tax efficient ways to save. You can put up to £15,240 a year into an Individual Savings Account (or ISA). ISAs have been around since the 1990s, but the limit on how much you can pay in, as well as the sorts of investments you can hold in one, have been relaxed over the years. Any interest or dividends you receive on investments in an ISA, as well as capital gains, are tax free.

The money we pay into our ISAs is out of income that has already been taxed. So with ISAs you pay the tax upfront, but do not have to pay anything extra when you withdraw the money and spend it. You also don't have to wait until retirement to take your money out, which makes ISAs more flexible. As we saw above, with pensions, you don't pay tax on the money you pay in, but you are taxed when you take it out. So there is a big difference in the tax advantages between an ISA and a personal pension.

So, which is better: an ISA or a pension? That's a good question, but a detailed answer depends on your individual circumstances. That means it is way beyond the scope of this book. Very roughly, ISAs are often appropriate near the start of your career. This is when you have a smaller salary and so have been subject to lower rates of tax on the income you pay into your ISA. You might also want to keep the flexibility of being able to get hold of the money you've saved in an emergency. If your career goes well, you will start paying higher rates of income tax. It might then be worth saving through a pension scheme because the tax you suffer on the earnings you pay into your pension will be added to your fund. You may also get help with pension contributions from your employer that depends on you paying in something as well.

Even without using an ISA or a pension scheme, the first £1,000 of interest we earn each year is exempt from tax (it's only £500 for higher rate taxpayers). We also get a £5,000 tax-free allowance for any dividends we receive. The net effect of these allowances is that very few people end up paying much tax on their savings.

How to live comfortably while paying almost no tax at all

All these encouragements to save, plus the way that capital gains tax and national insurance work, mean that living off your savings can be remarkably tax efficient. The drawback is that you need a good deal of money to start with. Let's step into the shoes of a wealthy couple called Mr and Mrs Rich. We're not talking about tax exiles or the super rich. Just a husband and wife with a few million in savings who like to live well but not extravagantly. Let's say they want an income of £120,000. This will keep them very comfortable, especially as they don't have a mortgage on their Georgian old rectory. The Riches live in the UK and all their income and savings are subject to UK tax. But they can still arrange their tax affairs to pay very little tax.

We'll compare the tax position of Mr and Mrs Rich to Alex Striver, who has the same gross income of £120,000, but who earns this substantial salary from her job.

To start with, Alex pays national insurance contributions of 12% on the first £40,000 or so of her earnings and 2% on the rest. Her employer has to pay NICs of another 13.8% on her salary. Alex's earnings of £120,000 a year mean a total national insurance bill (both employees' and employers') of £21,174. As for Mr and Mrs Rich, as all their income comes from their savings, they pay no national insurance. Not a groat. Admittedly, this means that they are not entitled to a state pension or unemployment benefits, but they really don't care about that. We've already seen that, as a market transaction, the state pension is a bad deal.

Still, Mr and Mrs Rich do still need £120,000 a year to live on and, since they aren't involved in any dodgy avoidance, their income tax bill should be exactly the same as Alex's. Or should it? Alex is working hard all day to earn £120,000 and she pays income tax of £41,200 a year on top of her national insurance. But with a bit of planning, the Riches can get their tax bill down to just a few thousand.

First of all, Mr and Mrs Rich arrange their affairs so that rather than one of them having an income of £120,000 they each receive

£60,000. They can easily do this by sharing their investments between them. Transferring shares, property and other assets between spouses has no tax effect. It means that they can use both of their tax-free allowances of £11,000 in full and ensure that much of the rest of their income is taxed at the basic rate of 20% instead of the higher rate of 40%. This simple step alone reduces their combined tax income bill from £41,200 to £26,400.

So far, the idle Riches have saved almost £36,000 of tax and national insurance compared to a worker with the same gross income. But £26,400 is still a lot of tax. Luckily for them, the Riches can also avail themselves of tax-advantaged savings products like ISAs. Like all of us, they can contribute up to £15,240 a year into an ISA (that's over £30,000 between them). Paying money into their ISAs doesn't reduce their taxable income, but the income and gains on the money they've saved in it are tax free. We can all take advantage of ISAs but, for the Riches, there is a crucial difference. When we pay money into an ISA, we can't then spend it. We can only save what we don't need to live on. But the Riches have a few million in the bank. For them, topping up their ISAs is just a matter of moving funds from one bank account to another. Despite the way ISAs are of most benefit to those with plenty of ready cash, the government has increased the annual limit to £20,000 from April 2017.

As it happens, the Riches have been paying the maximum amount into their ISAs for years (and before that, their predecessors with various acronyms like PEPs (Personal Equity Plans) and TESSAs (Tax Exempt Special Savings Accounts)). This means that they'll have a sizeable pool of tax-free savings and investments. From the time PEPs were introduced in 1987, they could have paid £455,400 into their tax-advantaged accounts. Including the growth in these investments over the years, this should generate tax-free income of over £25,000 a year if sensibly invested in corporate bond funds or similar.

The allowances for dividends and interest, which total £12,000 between them, provide the Riches with another tranche of tax-free income. They also each get a tax-free personal allowance of

£11,000. Finally, like everyone else, both the Riches have a £11,100 capital gains tax allowance. That means that they can make tax-free capital gains of £22,200 a year by selling some of their investments. In summary, the various allowances and exemptions give the Riches £81,200 of tax-free income a year. That leaves them with taxable receipts of £19,400 each and a combined tax bill of just £7,760. That compares to the £62,374 of income tax and national insurance that Alex and her employer pay on her earnings each year. Or, to put it another way, the Riches between them pay the same amount of tax as a worker on £26,300, slightly below the average wage (Table 3.1).

The Riches can arrange that they suffer even less tax, while still having £120,000 to spend each year, through judicious management of their share portfolio. What they need to do is sell their less successful investments at a loss and set that loss against gains they make on other share sales. To see this is worth doing, it is important to understand how the stock market works. A good rule of thumb for successful investing is to hold shares for the long term that are

Table 3.1 Comparing the taxes paid on wages and savings

	Income	Tax payable
Alex:	£	£
Employees' national insurance		5,733
Employers' national insurance		15,441
Income tax on salary	120,000	41,200
	120,000	62,374
The Riches:		
Personal allowances	22,000	-
Income tax on dividends	10,000	-
Income tax on interest	2,000	-
Income from ISAs	25,000	-
Capital gains allowances	22,200	-
Other income	38,800	7,760
	120,000	7,760

increasing and sell those that have lost value. Unfortunately, many amateur investors get this completely wrong. They cash in their gains and hold onto the bad performers in the hope that they will make good the loss. But Mr and Mrs Rich are not naive. When a share is doing consistently badly, they cut their losses and sell it. And each time they lose money, they get a capital loss for tax purposes. They can hang onto this and use it against profits from selling other shares. They expect, in the long term, to make net gains on their share portfolio and they can set their pool of capital losses against any gains that arise. Best of all, they can trigger capital gains and losses as they need them, then repurchase the shares they want to continue holding a few days later. This means that the Riches can generate all the cash they require from buying and selling shares without ever having to pay any tax on their capital gains. In practice, they will end up with some taxable income because the dividends on all their shareholdings are likely to exceed their tax-free allowances. But the resulting tax will be a fraction of what they would have paid had they worked to earn the same amount of money. And, if they do happen to accrue some taxable income by mistake, they can donate it tax free to cultural charities and enjoy the associated perks (not to mention the warm feeling inside), such as private viewings at the Royal Academy or priority booking for the opera.

Let's remind ourselves of the figures. Alex is very fortunate to earn £120,000 from her job. But she is hit by a tax bill for income tax and national insurance, plus the NICs payable by her employer, of £62,374. Mr and Mrs Rich don't work. Their combined tax bill on £120,000 is at most the same as that of a worker on the average wage and a little over a tenth of Alex's. It seems that if you have enough money that you don't need to work, you don't have to pay much tax either. In the UK as a whole, 92% of investment income, £79 billion in all, goes to just 10% of taxpayers, making it much more skewed towards the rich than earnings from work.

If this seems unfair, the hard question is what to do about it. One answer might be to combine national insurance and income tax so we all pay the same amount. Except that, in practice, Mr and Mrs

Rich are likely to be a retired couple whose wealth has been earned through having a successful career. Simply ordering pensioners, even wealthy pensioners, to pay national insurance would be a suicidal policy for any government. As we've noted before, pensioners have votes and they know how to use them.

Another idea might be to restrict the income tax reliefs available for losses and especially charitable donations. George Osborne did try to do just that in the 2012 budget. The trouble was that charities kicked up merry hell because they expected to lose donations. Mr Osborne had to execute a U-turn that contributed to the infamous 'omnishambles' episode. The government did manage to introduce some restrictions on income tax relief that do bite on the wallets of the seriously loaded. However, none of the planning I suggested above for Mr and Mrs Rich is affected.

We've already seen that a wealth tax, tempting though that is, suffers from a plethora of problems. Perhaps a better solution would be to bring in a 'minimum tax rate' of the kind that exists in some countries, including the USA. A minimum tax rate applies to people whose income is over a certain limit, so they always pay some tax regardless of the allowances and reliefs that they could otherwise claim. The government could also stop cutting income tax, which applies to everyone, and start cutting national insurance contributions instead, which would only benefit people in work.

Given how much attention we pay to the fairness of the tax system, it is a surprise to find out just how unfairly it discriminates against work and encourages sloth. But in the short term, it is difficult to see what to do about it.

4

Taxes on business

Taxing business

Business is the way that a country makes its way in the world. We need businesses to generate the money and provide most of the goods and services that we consume day by day. Almost all businesses are in the private sector and they range from sole traders, such as a man with a van or a self-employed gardener, all the way up to the largest companies, like the oil giant BP and the pharmaceuticals leviathan GlaxoSmithKline.

Much of the money that businesses make is spent on paying the people who work for them. That's as true for a self-employed builder (who is only paying himself) as it is for the biggest multinationals. We noted in Chapter 1 how businesses pay over the income tax and national insurance on our salaries to the government. And in Chapter 2 we saw that businesses are also responsible for collecting VAT (although we are the ones who pay it). But the administration of these taxes is no doddle and it is firms that have to pay the penalties if they mess it up. The UK's tax collection system has effectively been privatised. While HMRC is nominally responsible, it has subcontracted most of the donkey work. Getting businesses to pay our taxes for us has the advantage of ensuring that we stay largely ignorant of just how much we pay. It's the Third Golden Rule, keeping taxes invisible, in action.

Tax on the self-employed and small businesses

If you are self-employed, the taxman will charge income tax and national insurance on all your earnings from your business after deducting expenses. You end up paying about the same amount of tax as you would if you were being paid a salary equal to your profits by an employer. There are a couple of advantages to self-employment. You pay slightly lower national insurance and don't have to pay employers' NICs. (Although you do have to cough up a small extra amount of national insurance called Class 2 contributions of about £145 a year. This trivial and fiddly tax is due for abolition.) You also don't always have to pay the tax you owe immediately. Sometimes you can defer the tax on your profits for 20 months after you have earned them.

If the self-employed want to reinvest their profits to help grow the business, paying half of them away in income tax and national insurance is unhelpful. Luckily, businesses can also deduct the first £200,000 of investment (on computers, machinery and other capital equipment) from their taxable profits. So even when a successful small firm is growing, money ploughed back into the business is often tax free.

To be honest, for many small businesses, income tax is the least of their worries. They only pay it if they are making profits and that makes it a nice problem to have. That's not to say tax isn't a serious issue for small firms. But the one that keeps shopkeepers and entrepreneurs awake at night is business rates. These are the commercial equivalent of council tax. Like council tax, rates go to fund local government. A total of £26 billion a year is collected and, through a complicated formula, it is redistributed to local authorities. Unlike council tax, business rates are not automatically spent in the same area that they were collected and councils don't even get much say on what the level should be. Going forward, local authorities will get to keep increases in the revenue from business rates in their patch, but conversely they are on the hook if they do not manage to collect enough.

The trouble with rates is the way they are levied. To figure out how much to pay, a business first needs to know the theoretical amount that someone would pay to rent the premises it occupies. This 'rateable value' is determined during a regular exercise by the valuation office agency. The business has to pay roughly half of this amount as a tax each year. It doesn't matter if the business is doing well or seriously struggling. And the tax is also unfair in the way that it hits some kinds of trade harder than others. A boutique in an upmarket part of Islington might not make much money selling hand woven alpaca cardigans to discerning members of the intelligentsia. But the high business rates it has to pay reflect the fact that its shop is in a gentrified area even though being a purveyor of attire to hipsters isn't very profitable. Conversely, a small office in an out-of-town development might contain a few highly paid executives for whom the business rates are not a significant cost.

In short, business rates are oppressive for a retailer who has to locate close to its customers. One result is that charity shops, which get an 80% rebate on business rates, have colonised high streets where regular stores are priced out. The government periodically promises a review of business rates, but the chance of serious reform founders on the need to raise the same amount of money after any changes.

Tax on companies

Profits made by companies are not subject to income tax or national insurance contributions. Instead, they have to pay corporation tax which is charged on profits, not sales or turnover. When the newspapers are reporting on the tax affairs of a company and want to make out they are not paying enough tax, they will often report the company's turnover (i.e. the total amount that the company sells) and the corporation tax they pay (which is probably much lower). However, this can be misleading. A company could have an enormous turnover but only manage to make a loss. The online retailer

Amazon is a case in point. In 2014, it had worldwide sales of $89 billion, but contrived to lose $241 million. In that case, it shouldn't have to pay any corporation tax. And tax is not even calculated on a company's published bottom line or the profits before tax disclosed in the financial statements. Instead it is a percentage of its taxable profits, which are derived from the accounts but subject to all sorts of adjustments.

Tax accountants like me, who have spent their entire careers working on corporation tax, tend to overestimate its importance to real people. But, although it brings in about £44 billion a year and accounts for 8% of government receipts, the fact it is only charged on profits makes it much less resented than business rates. The real reason that accountants devote so much time to corporation tax is that it is so complicated. Almost all companies need professional advice to figure out how much they have to pay, and that is a nice little earner for us bean-counters.

At first sight, corporation tax seems to break the Second Golden Rule: 'No matter what name is on the bill, all taxes are ultimately suffered by human beings.' After all, companies are taxed on their profits rather than on the money they pay to their employees and directors. If corporation tax is levied on a company's profits, does this really mean that it breaks the second rule? No. As we saw when we looked at pension funds in the previous chapter, it turns out that corporation tax isn't really suffered by companies. Like other taxes, it is levied on people. To understand how this can be, consider what a company can do with its profits. First, it can pay them out as dividends to its shareholders. If those shareholders are people, they have to pay income tax on the dividends they receive. Corporation tax is just a down payment on the tax paid by shareholders.

The other thing a company can do with its profits is invest them in growing its business. In other words, corporation tax is a tax on investment. Directly taxing the investment the country desperately needs to improve productivity is not a terribly good idea.

Most politicians realise this, which is why the rate of corporation tax has been cut from 30% in 2007 to 20% from 2015, and will be

17% in 2020. It was 52% in the 1970s. But given taxing companies makes so little sense economically, why do it? There are several reasons why we probably won't see corporation tax cut to zero. First, not all shareholders pay tax. We've seen that dividends received by pension funds aren't taxed. So, it is only by taxing company profits that the government gets a cut.

Then there is also the matter of foreign multinationals that make plenty of profit in the UK but whose shareholders mainly live elsewhere. Corporation tax is a way for the British government to obtain a portion of these firms' UK profits before they pay them over to their foreign head offices.

Personal service companies

Another reason corporation tax will never be abolished is that it's an example of a 'bookend tax', rather like capital gains tax. If corporation tax were too low, there would be a massive incentive for everyone to run their affairs through a company rather than being self-employed. In fact, plenty of people already work through personal service companies. As we saw above, if you are self-employed, you have to pay income tax and national insurance contributions. But suppose, instead, that you formed a company and ran your business through that. Your personal service company hires you out to whoever you want to work for. You'd then only pay 20% corporation tax on your profits. When you want to spend the money, you need your company to pay you a dividend. However, dividends are taxed at a lower rate to take into account the corporation tax already paid by the company. Better still, you can give half the shares in your company to your spouse to take advantage of both your personal allowances and double your combined income before either of you have to pay income tax at a higher rate. Best of all, no one pays any national insurance.

Understandably, HMRC is perturbed by all this. It has brought in various rules to make sure only people who are genuinely running their own businesses can use a personal service company. If you are a consultant but you do all your work for one client, HMRC may try to claim you are really employed by the client. This would mean that you would be subject to PAYE on anything you were paid while your client would have to pay employers' national insurance. The leaflet on all this published by HMRC is called IR35 and it has achieved a certain amount of notoriety.

Among the people paid through personal service companies were several well-known TV personalities. Actors tend to be genuinely self-employed. Most of them have to take any work they can and few, even some who are quite familiar faces, make very much money. They might be doing a voiceover for an advertising agency one day and a cameo in a detective drama the next. In these circumstances, it is hard for HMRC to argue that they are employed by anyone but themselves. If they want to work through a personal service company, increasing their administration costs but probably saving some tax, that's up to them. For someone who is exclusively contracted to the BBC, the situation is rather different. When Jeremy Paxman, whose day job is presenting University Challenge and who, at the time, was also frontman for Newsnight, revealed he was being paid through a personal service company, the BBC were embarrassed. The print media, always happy to stick the boot into the Beeb and its highly paid talent, kicked up a fuss. After some procrastination, the BBC agreed that it wouldn't sign any new contracts with personal service companies. The net effect of the BBC employing its staff directly is probably that TV stars will demand to be paid a bit more money and the licence fee will be slightly higher to compensate.

HMRC has had considerable success squeezing more money out of the self-employed by treating them as being employed by someone else. They did, however, suffer a major setback in the courts when they tried to deal with companies where a husband and wife are the major shareholders. As we saw in Chapter 3, it can be tax efficient for couples to allocate their assets between themselves so that the total income of the family is split up. This can keep the combined earnings of the family out of a higher tax bracket.

Mr and Mrs Geoff Jones arranged their affairs in that way. Mr Jones was an IT contractor who ran his business through a personal service company. He owned roughly half the shares and Mrs Jones held the other half. Mrs Jones also helped out with the administration of the business. HMRC claimed that the dividends Mrs Jones received from the company really belonged to Mr Jones, so he should pay income tax on them at the higher rate. In 2007, the case went all the way to the House of Lords, which, at that time, was the highest court in the land. The taxman lost. Effectively, the Law Lords decided that the rules let married couples share their assets as they saw fit. And there was nothing the taxman could do about it.

The reaction of the government to the victory of Mr and Mrs Jones was to threaten new laws that would reverse the decision. Luckily, good sense prevailed and the plans were quickly shelved. Of course, if you want to arrange your own affairs in a similar way to the Jones's, you must take professional advice. Get it even slightly wrong and the taxman will take a substantial bite from your funds, as several other couples have found.

By the way, the judgment in favour of Mr and Mrs Jones was delivered by Lord Hoffmann, probably one of the best known judges of recent years. It was his failure to declare his connection to Amnesty International that led to his fellow Law Lords overturning his decision to send the late Chilean dictator Augusto Pinochet to Spain for trial in 1998. Despite this catastrophic error, Lord Hoffmann was a good judge for tax cases. He was clever enough to understand the complicated issues even though he was not a tax specialist. He also tried to use his judgments to make the law clearer. This clarity means his words are often quoted by tax lawyers. Lord Hoffmann has now retired and the shortage of senior judges with a background in tax law is a critical problem. Very few of the leading tax silks ever become judges. This is partly because they have to take a hefty pay cut when they join the bench. But judges are also expected to be generalists. Tax is so specialised that it is hard for people whose professional lives have been dedicated to this one area to gain the necessary level of expertise across the board. The paucity of judicial experience in tax has led to some poor judgments by the higher courts written by judges who may not have grasped all the subtleties of the relevant law.

Luckily, all tax cases are first heard by specialist tax tribunals before they even reach the higher courts. The judges at these tribunals are often tax lawyers who definitely do know their onions. This is helpful but it means we have the absurd position that the junior judges are better qualified than the senior ones. At the moment, only a single member of the Court of Appeal and none of the Supreme Court panel is a tax specialist. The sooner more tax lawyers are tempted onto the bench, the better for justice and perhaps also for a bit more precision in tax law.

The tradesman's entrance

If you are self-employed or a freelance consultant, you will already be aware that you have to fill in a tax return to record your business earnings. You might have considered incorporating so you can run your business through a company. You might even have done so already. But a lot of people are in business without even realising it. And these people are a special target for the taxman as they may be paying less tax than they should.

Could you be one? We saw in Chapter 3 how buying a clapped out old motor to restore and sell on at a profit is taxable. Someone buying and selling cigarette cards, or growing vegetables for a stall at the local farmers' market, could be caught too. Foster carers are another category of people who may not realise that looking after deprived and abused children is taxable. The question you have to ask is, have your activities gone beyond a casual hobby? In tax lingo, have you started to trade? Accountants spend a good deal of their time figuring out whether an activity is a trade or not. There have been lots of court cases and even a royal commission on the question.

A few decades ago, being in trade was looked down upon by the upper classes. For all I know, it still is. If you are a doctor, lawyer or accountant you can be just as self-employed as a second-hand car dealer but, for a long time, professional vocations were taxed separately from traders. The amount payable was identical, but plumbers and professionals were hermetically sealed into distinct classes. This institutional snobbery didn't disappear until 2005, long after it had become completely pointless.

As far as HMRC is concerned, if you are trading, you need to pay income tax and national insurance as if you are self-employed. A particular target is eBay. Flogging off a few unwanted gadgets is unlikely to be a trade and probably isn't taxable. But if you are buying things in order to sell them on eBay and hoping to turn a profit, then that sounds a lot more like a trade and HMRC will be interested.

Even business of dubious legality is subject to tax. Providing an escort service is more likely to attract the attention of the tax authorities than the local vice squad. For example, in 2012, Donna Asutaits, described as a high-class call girl, was jailed for evading £120,000 in tax. And, as everyone knows, the notorious gangster Al Capone was eventually convicted of tax fraud rather than for any of his various other misdemeanours, including ordering many murders. We'll look more closely at tax evasion and why it is such a bad idea in the next chapter.

In deciding if you are engaged in a taxable trade, profit motive is a key point. If you are simply doing something for fun and don't realistically expect to make any money, it is much harder for the taxman to argue that you are trading. Writing a novel in your spare time is a good example of something that is unlikely to be a trade. Deep down inside, you know that the chance of it being published commercially is pretty small. And if you self-publish, it's unlikely to be read by anyone but your family and close friends (if that). You are probably not trading. If you do make money from the venture, you will still have to pay income tax on any royalties, but not national insurance. On the other hand, an eBay trader or someone renting out a room on Airbnb may need to register with HMRC. If their profits exceed £6,000 they may need to start paying national insurance. And if they have a job as well, profits from trading are added to their salary for tax purposes and they pay tax at their highest marginal rate. All of which means, if you think you might be trading, it is worth getting some professional advice or calling an HMRC helpline.

However, with ever more people being drawn into the business tax net from small-scale ventures on the internet, the government has now taken action to make sure most of them won't have to trouble HMRC. From the tax year beginning in April 2017, everyone will be allowed to make up to £1,000 a year from each of trading and renting without paying tax on it.

Multinationals and international tax

When it comes to tax, the media are more interested in big business than the self-employed. So let's look at how we tax the profits of the multinational companies who are headquartered or make their money in the UK. Are they really gaming the system?

At the time of writing, the world's most valuable publicly traded company is Alphabet Inc., the parent company of Google, which is worth about $550 billion. It has a turnover of $75 billion, comparable to the gross domestic product of Cuba and Oman. However, unlike these countries, big corporations such as Alphabet Inc. are theoretically accountable to their shareholders, who get to vote on how the company is run. Most of the shares are controlled by big institutional investors like pension funds, who are more likely to just sell their shares if they are unhappy with how things are going than to actively influence the company. That makes companies look like invincible monoliths under the control of no one. But that isn't true. Even the most enormous multinationals are more vulnerable than they appear. Economists have noted that of the biggest 500 companies in the USA 40 years ago, only 74 are still in the rankings.

The rest, 85% of them, have been gobbled up, gone bust or faded into insignificance. It's the same across the world. Companies as famous as Pan Am, Saab and Lehman Brothers are no more. Brands that were recently ubiquitous like Blackberry, Nokia, AOL and Yahoo are shadows of their former selves, pushed aside by Apple, Samsung and Google. Even mighty Microsoft faces a less certain future than it seemed to a few years ago.

So the idea that multinationals are immortal leviathans in control of the world is fantasy. They are vulnerable to changes in fashion and must operate within the law. The ones that don't, like Enron, can collapse like a house of cards as soon as they are found out. That said, big business is extremely important. It's not just the jobs created by these companies that benefit us. The ancillary work done by lawyers, consultants and other professionals is just as important. This might not be very glamorous, but these are good jobs that any responsible government has a duty to promote. Multinationals also keep the country supplied with many of the goods, services and infrastructure we have come to depend on.

Even though we need them, it is tempting to imagine that the government could realistically extract vast amounts of additional taxes from multinationals. Judging by what we read in the newspapers, some people think of multinationals as money trees just waiting to be plundered. MPs like Labour's shadow Chancellor John McDonnell, as well as pressure groups like the Tax Justice Network and UK Uncut, have been vocal in their demands that big business pay its 'fair share'. For example, in 2012, it was revealed that the coffee chain Starbucks had paid no corporation tax since 2009 and precious little over previous years. UK Uncut staged protests at some of its ubiquitous cafes, attracting a good deal of media attention. Starbucks, founded in the liberal city of Seattle on the US west coast in 1971, has always seen itself as the acceptable face of capitalism. The protests were a shock to its management, who took the unusual step of volunteering to pay £20 million of tax in 2013 and 2014. Unfortunately, this was taken as an admission of guilt by the public and reinforced their reputation as tax avoiders.

If it was possible, any sensible government would squeeze as much as it could from big business. After all, if it could get multinationals (who don't have votes) to pay the lion's share of tax, it would win every election. Sadly, life is not that simple. This isn't really a party-political point. The corporate tax policy of the last Labour government was not very different to that of the present Conservative government. Although the Coalition and Conservative governments have extended some of Labour's reforms, they have followed the blueprint laid down while Labour was still in power. It is worth explaining what that policy is, and why it is probably sensible.

Territorial taxes

The UK charges tax on profits that companies make in the UK. That means that even when a multinational is based here, it only pays corporation tax on the money it makes locally. Its business in any other country is no matter for the British taxman. If BP is drilling for oil in the USA or Vodafone is selling mobile phone contracts in Switzerland, the UK won't try to tax any of the profits that result. Multinationals can pay their global profits back to their UK headquarters and distribute them as dividends to their shareholders without incurring any UK corporation tax. However, BP's activities in the North Sea and Vodafone's in Watford high street fall within the UK tax net. Any profits that companies make on activities in Britain are subject to corporation tax.

Just taxing profits that arise within a country's own borders is called a 'territorial' system and most major jurisdictions now operate in this way. Each country gets to tax profits made in its own territory but not in anyone else's. The UK was one of the last major economies to move from a worldwide system (where companies paid UK tax on their global profits) to a territorial one. Of the major advanced economies, only the USA persists with a global system and it is under huge pressure to change as well. For a long time, the sclerotic political system in Washington prevented this from happening. However, with Donald Trump's victory in the November 2016 election, the Republican Party now controls both houses of congress and the presidency, so plans to force through radical tax reform. In contrast to the treatment of companies, when it comes to income tax, most countries tax the worldwide income of all their residents.

From the point of view of the UK, a territorial tax system has several advantages. The most significant is that it means a multinational can base itself here, with all the jobs and investment that entails, without having to pay UK tax on its international activities. If every country has a territorial system, what matters is keeping tax rates low and ensuring that governments allow free movement of capital in and out. The USA is facing serious problems with its worldwide tax system because many of its multinationals are trying to escape to other countries. This is what the US pharmaceuticals giant Pfizer was doing when it wanted to merge with the UK drugs company AstraZeneca in 2014. Any commercial issues were purely ancillary to the tax advantages. Other US corporations use elaborate tax schemes to prevent their overseas profits from being taxed back in the USA.

There is little doubt (and no secret) that the UK has made a virtue out of the necessity of having a territorial tax system. Seeing the way the wind was blowing, both Labour and Conservative governments have tried to make our tax regime as attractive to business as possible. And it's working. Despite Brexit, lots of groups are moving their headquarters to the UK. Meanwhile, the USA has brought in emergency regulations to prevent any more of its major companies escaping across the Atlantic.

Having multinationals based here in the UK is good for the economy. Nonetheless, 'tax justice' pressure groups have been angered by what they perceive as unfair practices by these big companies. In some cases, they might have a point. As more thoughtful campaigners, like ex-tax inspector Richard Brooks, have pointed out, the big multinationals are owned by shareholders in rich countries like the USA and the UK. That's where their profits end up. If a multinational avoids taxes in a developing country, it is effectively transferring wealth from a poor part of the world to a rich one. For Brooks, developing countries are being short-changed by multinationals not paying tax locally. It also distorts competition when some companies cut their tax bills through aggressive planning while others don't. There is either a race to the bottom as all businesses try to avoid all the taxes that they can, or the ones who don't are put at a competitive disadvantage.

Tax havens

The challenge of a territorial system is making sure that profits made in the UK are taxed in the UK, while profits made in Botswana are taxed in Botswana. And some companies have become adept at shifting profits out of the territory in which they belong into tax havens or even making them disappear altogether. That means profits generated in the UK can end up being taxed somewhere else or not at all. As businesses have become more global and tax systems have become more territorial, this problem has been growing.

When you think of a tax haven, you probably imagine somewhere like Monaco or Liechtenstein. Or perhaps a warm desert island like the Cayman or British Virgin Islands. These are all tax havens and everyone knows it. This is a problem for them. While the UK only taxes profits made in the UK, it makes an exception for tax havens. If a company is holding its investments in somewhere like the Cayman Islands for no good reason, the UK will tax them as if they were really in the UK. Many respectable countries also slap taxes on any interest or dividends paid to these tax havens since they assume that the only reason anyone would set up there is to avoid or evade taxes. For example, pay a dividend from the USA to the Cayman Islands and the US government will take 30 cents of every dollar as a withholding tax.

Countries like the UK, France and Japan, which have real economies and proper tax systems, don't get hit nearly so badly by these withholding taxes. This is because, starting after the Second World War, they have agreed tax treaties with each other. These are bilateral agreements under which, among other things, they agree to charge only reduced or zero rates of withholding tax. So when a US corporation pays a dividend to the UK, there is no withholding tax. The same is the case with treaties between most other countries in the world. The UK has one of the widest treaty networks of all, from Argentina to Zambia, making it a good place to base international operations.

But what happens when a tax haven pretends to be a respectable country, so it has a wide treaty network? Well, we can always cancel the treaty next time it comes up for renewal. The trouble for the UK is that some of the best tax havens in the world are members of the European Union: in particular Luxembourg. It may not be entirely coincidental that Amazon bases its European operations in Luxembourg, together with many other high-tech groups. Recently, the European Commission has begun to investigate whether some big multinationals have been getting special treatment from the Luxembourg government. Progress had been slow, but when details of deals that multinationals could cut with the Luxembourg authorities were leaked to the newspapers in 2014, the Grand Duchy belatedly attempted to clean up its act. At the same time, other members of the EU, such as Ireland, have been modernising their tax systems to make it more difficult for corporate profits to disappear into the Atlantic mists.

A bit of BEPS

More widely, the G20 club of major rich nations, working with other groups like the EU and the OECD, are engaged in a major project to make sure that profits are taxed in the right territory. The motive force for this initiative came from former British Prime

Minister David Cameron, but there is little doubt he was influenced by grassroots tax justice campaigns. The overarching project, managed out of the OECD's offices in Paris, goes by the unsexy name of Base Erosion and Profit Shifting, or BEPS for short. The aim is to reach a series of international agreements to ensure that multinationals are taxed in the countries where they actually make their money: in other words, to prevent profits from being shifted out of one country into another. The other element of the project is to combat base erosion. This is when companies use differences or gaps between tax systems to make profits disappear altogether, thus reducing their tax base in the territories in which they operate.

The difference the BEPS project will make in the long term still isn't clear. Many countries, including the UK, are taking it extremely seriously. However, the attitude of the USA is still uncertain. Given that various oddities of the US tax system are among the main reasons that base erosion is possible in the first place, the full benefits of the BEPS project may have to wait for domestic US tax reform. That might be a while coming.

In the meantime, the British government has been taking unilateral action to deal with international tax avoidance. In March 2015, it introduced a brand new impost called diverted profits tax. This is designed to catch profits that multinationals make from UK activities that are being booked outside the UK. It has been nicknamed the 'Google tax' because Google is one company alleged to be avoiding UK taxes in this way. The government wants diverted profits tax to encourage companies to move their profits out of tax havens and back into the UK where they can be subject to corporation tax. So, if the new tax is successful, no one will pay it because all the profits to which it is intended to apply will have been voluntarily returned to the UK. Also, in 2017, the UK is implementing elements of the BEPS project designed to prevent multinationals from exploiting mismatches between different countries' tax regimes to cut their bills, as well as restricting the amount of interest for which companies can claim tax deductions.

One of the major challenges of taxing multinationals is the way they split their activities up between lots of different places. They might do this for commercial reasons, but it makes it hard to decide how much profit should be taxed at each location. The digital economy, which enables people to do business in a country without ever setting foot there, is another complication. The method used to allocate the correct profits to be taxed in each country is called transfer pricing. While this is not a concept many people come across in everyday life, it is central to the taxation of cross-border business.

Where does big business make its profits?

If you happen to be reading this book on an iPad, turn it over. On the back, it says 'Designed by Apple in California' and 'Assembled in China'. To that terse message we could probably add 'Sold in the UK'. So where does the profit from an iPad properly end up: the USA, China or the UK? Everyone knows that Apple is fantastically profitable, but only when you know in which country the profits were made can you decide which government gets to tax them.

Taxing the profits made from physically constructing an iPad is easy. Apple pays manufacturers in the Far East to produce the components for its products and to put them together. The amount Apple agrees to pay Taiwan electronics giant Foxconn to assemble an iPad is just the market price for that service. The reason we know that is because Apple and Foxconn are independent enterprises. Foxconn makes electronics for Samsung and other firms as well. It will accept a fee from Apple such that it makes a reasonable profit, while Apple won't pay more than it has to. In tax jargon, Apple and Foxconn are acting at arm's length. Foxconn makes all the profits from building the iPad in its factory in China and is subject to tax there. We'll see how transactions which are not at arm's length can be manipulated to minimise taxes below.

What happens when you buy an iPad? Let's say you bought yours in London. If you buy an iPad from Currys, Apple isn't even a party to the sale. You and the retailer are both acting at arm's length again. Apple does have various ways to prevent retailers from offering discounts on its products (so you almost never see an iPad at a sale price), but these have nothing to do with tax.

It's important to note that Apple doesn't necessarily make any UK profits selling iPads to Currys at wholesale. This is because all Apple have done is hire a shipping company to import the completed devices from China to the UK. So, despite the fact that Apple sells billions of pounds of products in the UK, they might make very little of its profits here. Instead, Currys is taxed in the UK on the money it makes from selling Apple's products.

There's been some press coverage, both here and elsewhere, about how little Apple pays in tax in countries like the UK and Australia. This coverage is based on the mistaken belief that because consumers in the UK buy products from overseas, the British government has a right to a slice of the foreign companies' profits. In fact, when someone in Hartlepool buys a new Volkswagen, the profit from designing and building the car is made in Germany and taxed there. The converse is also true. When Aga sells one of its up-market ovens to someone in Denmark, the profits remain in the UK. That is one reason why exports are good for the economy.

So where does Apple make its money? I can give you the address. It's One Infinite Loop, Cupertino, California. That's where the brains' trust resides. Sir Jony Ive, Tim Cook and, above all, the spirit of the late Steve Jobs are found there. So we'd expect that Apple would pay the lion's share of its taxes in the USA. And indeed they do.

The way Apple figures out exactly where it should book its profits is through the special technique of transfer pricing. A great deal of the heat over international taxation is generated over the way this works. So it is worth considering transfer pricing in a bit more detail. I'll keep using an iPad as my example, but I should point out that I have no idea about the numbers that Apple really uses in transfer prices for its products.

Let's say you have to pay £399 for a new iPad when you buy it from Currys. That is the VAT inclusive price. With VAT at 20% going to the British government, the net price of an iPad is just £330. And of that, Currys might make £50 as its retailer's margin. That means Apple sells iPads to UK retailers for £280. Out of that £280, Apple has to get the iPad built and shipped to the UK. It also needs to pay for its excellent customer service. This is run out of Ireland, as is most of its European sales and administration. And it requires money for the research and development of its products in California. On top of that, Apple wants to make a profit.

As we've already seen, the amount Apple pays Foxconn to build an iPad is called an arm's length price. The cost of transporting the product to the UK will be at arm's length too because the shipping company is independent of Apple. Let's assume it cost £150 to manufacture and then transport an iPad to the UK. If Apple sells it to a retailer for £280, as we have assumed, the company is left with revenue of £130 per iPad. Although the money comes from your wallet in the UK, we noted above that most of it belongs in California and Ireland.

Splitting the £130 of revenue fairly between Ireland (for the administration, sales and customer service) and the USA is not straightforward. The correct way to do it is to imagine that Apple's Irish operations are not really run by Apple. Instead, we pretend an independent company, which we could call Pear Limited, does all the things that Apple actually does in Ireland. Pear Limited also wants to make a profit for itself, which, because it is an Irish company, will be taxable in Ireland. What we have to ask is, how much would Apple need to pay Pear for it to carry out Apple's Irish sales and administration functions, as well as make a reasonable profit? Because we are pretending Pear is not connected to Apple, that amount must be an arm's length price. Unfortunately, figuring out what the arm's length price should be is difficult. And once you have worked it out, you have to persuade the local taxman that you are right. Luckily, accountancy firms have small armies of people who do nothing but transfer pricing all day. For a fee, they'll be happy to help out.

Let's assume that some transfer pricing boffins have worked out that a fair arm's length price for what the hypothetical company Pear Ltd does in Ireland is £40 per iPad. That means that Apple must recognise £40 of income in Ireland where it forms part of its Irish taxable profit. The rest of its revenue, being £90, belongs in California.

To recap where the £399 you spent on your iPad has gone (on the basis of my example numbers):

- £69 of VAT that went to the British government.
- £50 of margin for Currys that goes into its UK profits subject to corporation tax.
- Of the remaining £280, Apple pays Foxconn and the shipping company £150 to build and transport the iPad to the UK. That's taxed in the Far East.
- Apple keeps the remaining £130 of which £40 is allocated to Ireland and taxed there.
- Finally, the last £90 should be taxed in the USA.

What is the £90 of revenue attributable to the USA for? In short, it represents income from designing the iPad and for using the Apple name. When we buy an iPad, we are paying Apple for the rights to use its software, the Apple brand, the design of the stores and for a share of the worldwide marketing costs. And we have to pay Apple in Ireland for the helpful customer service and administrative support. These payments are all transfer prices and, if they are wrong, Apple will be taxed on its profits in the wrong places. The Internal Revenue Service in the USA will want to ensure that enough profits are transferred back to California. But the Irish Revenue and HMRC will be just as keen to ensure transfer pricing isn't used to illegitimately divert profits out of Ireland and the UK respectively. With national tax authorities pulling in different directions, it is hardly surprising that transfer pricing specialists have proliferated in the big accounting firms in recent years.

The figures above are just illustrations to show how the system works. The reality is likely to be far more complicated. But the concept is simple: figure out all the places where people are making money from designing, building or selling iPads. Then make sure that the profit each of these people makes is taxed in the country they are working in. When the companies involved are separate enterprises, like Currys, Apple and Foxconn, that is easy to do. But when a multinational has operations in lots of countries, it becomes a good deal more difficult. Nonetheless, for physical goods like cookers and computers, the system works reasonably well. Profits are generated where goods are designed and built. Profits from selling the items are made by retailers. It is fairly easy to tell where everyone is located and tax them accordingly.

Because transfer prices can be so difficult to determine, companies often agree them in advance with the tax authorities of the countries in which they operate. Advance transfer pricing agreements are a good idea because they provide certainty and mean businesses can plan ahead. Of course, these agreements need to be fair and objective. As it happens, the European Commission has investigated the advance transfer pricing agreement between Apple and the Irish tax authorities. The Commission thinks that the agreement gives Apple an unfair advantage over its competitors, something the company and the Irish tax authorities vehemently deny. If it turns out that they have been given a special deal, Apple would have to return any tax they have saved to the Irish government, going back ten years. The Commission thinks Apple should pay back the princely sum of €13 billion.

Tax competition

One of the main reasons that Apple has set up its European operations in Ireland is that the Irish corporation tax rate is just 12.5%, rather than 20% in the UK and 35% in the USA. Ireland's low taxes, coupled with an educated English-speaking population and close proximity to other European countries, mean that massive multinationals want to do business there. It is, more than anything else, this that has allowed Ireland to successfully bounce back from the financial crisis while Spain, Italy and Greece are still in the doldrums. Of course, there are reasons you might prefer to locate in Manchester or Milan rather than Cork. The social and shopping scenes are better, for a start. If you like football, you are better off based in Cheshire or Lombardy. And it rains in Ireland – a great deal more than the tourism advertisements would have you believe. Low corporation tax attracts business by compensating for other factors. Business means jobs. And jobs mean income tax and national insurance revenue, not to mention happy citizens. No wonder the UK has reduced its corporation tax rate by over a quarter in five years, from 28% to 20%. Following Brexit, it is due to drop all the way to 17% by 2020.

Having its global headquarters in California has definite advantages for Apple. Cupertino is close to the technological power house of Silicon Valley and the geek farms at the Universities of California and Berkeley. It also rains a good deal less than in Ireland. Despite these benefits, California also has a serious disadvantage as a place to establish a business. It suffers, in common with the rest of the USA, from an unusually high corporate tax rate. The US federal tax rate for companies is 35% and there is a 9% surcharge from the state of California itself. This comes to over twice the tax rate in the UK and three times that in Ireland. Far from avoiding tax in Britain, Apple would be a great deal better off if all its profits were taxed here rather than in the USA. Much of Apple's alleged tax planning that we read about in the newspapers is aimed at reducing the effect of the USA's high corporate tax rates. Nonetheless, Apple recognises more income in the USA than anywhere else and also pays more of its tax bill (a total of about $13 billion in 2015) to America's Internal Revenue Service than to any other tax authority.

That countries have radically different tax rates makes transfer pricing even more important. Suppose a multinational has operations in two countries: one with a corporate tax rate of 40% and one with a corporate tax rate of 20%. It obviously becomes worthwhile for it to ensure its profits are taxed in the country with the lower tax rate. We saw above how transfer pricing is used to make sure profits are allocated to the right country. But you could also set your transfer prices to deliberately move profits to countries with low tax rates at the expense of countries with high rates. And because transfer prices are so subjective and hard to determine accurately, there is a lot of room for debate as to what they should be. This is a huge issue for tax authorities around the world. HMRC has been involved in a number of intractable transfer pricing disputes with multinationals that have dragged on for years. The new diverted profits tax we noted above, introduced by George Osborne in 2015, is intended to strengthen the hand of HMRC in arguments over transfer pricing. A substantial part of the OECD's BEPS agenda is aimed at the same problem.

Transfer pricing is esoteric and complex. Most ordinary people haven't even heard of it. But I hope readers won't mind that I have devoted a few pages to the topic because it is the single most important issue in the world of international tax.

Taxing what you can't touch

What do you get when you buy an iPad? Of course, you get a physical object, which was assembled in China. More than that, you get the benefit of that object's design. It could have been made by any number of high tech manufacturers, but if it is an iPad it could only have been designed by Sir Jony Ive and his team in Cupertino. You also get the cachet of having an Apple tablet instead of one from Tesco. Even more significant is the computer software on your iPad, called iOS. This is 'free' in that you don't have to pay for it separately. But you really paid for the software as part of the cost when you bought the hardware. Access to the App Store, Apple customer service, not to mention iTunes and integration with a Mac computer or iPhone, if you have them, add icing to the cake. When you buy an iPad, you get the whole package. Most of the value is made up of ethereal things beyond the physical product. You can't touch these things so, for that reason, they are called 'intangible' assets by accountants, indirectly from the Latin *tango* meaning 'I touch'. The most common kind of intangible asset is intellectual property.

Intellectual property is the software on your computer; it accounts for the difference between a Christian Dior outfit and one from Topshop; it's the marketing, brands and design that go into almost every modern consumer product. Copyright is a typical example. You, the reader, may own a physical copy of this book. But I hold the copyright and receive a royalty payment each time a bookshop sells one. Businesses guard their intellectual property very carefully. For example, when in 2013 Bentley Motors found that a small outfit in Florida was selling body kits so that car owners could make their old banger look a bit like a Continental GTC, they sued. The judge found for Bentley because its trademarks and rights to designs (two kinds of intellectual property) had been infringed.

Obviously, it is easy to transfer intellectual property across borders and that makes it a headache for the tax system. Businesses can base their brands, copyrights and other intangible assets in tax havens so that the royalties they receive are not subject to tax. As a result, the UK and other countries have rules to prevent intellectual property being moved offshore and to tax the resulting royalties even if they are paid to a tax haven. These special rules are the stick that the taxman uses to extract the tax on intangibles. But lots of countries, including the UK, also deploy a carrot in the form of incentives to attract intangibles to their shores and into their tax nets.

Governments are forever trying to encourage particular activities with tax incentives. In the olden days, things were more transparent. Ministers would pick favoured industries and pay them subsidies. Unfortunately, this policy was often a disaster for the industries concerned. They learnt to rely on governmental liberality and lost competitiveness as a result. Margaret Thatcher usually gets the credit, or blame, for putting a stop to subsidies, but it was the EU that made them illegal. Nowadays, the government disguises its payments and delivers them through the tax system.

In the UK and many other countries, there are special tax breaks for the innovation needed to create intellectual property. For example, if you are a small business and spend £100 on research, you can reduce your taxable profits by £230. Naturally, if you don't have any profits (as is often the case at the early stage of a product's development) the tax deduction isn't much use. So the government will instead pay you a cash sum nearly equal to the tax you would have saved if you had any profits. Now, the technical term for money paid to companies that aren't making any money is a subsidy, but tax credit sounds so much more wholesome. Although the EU is supposed to forbid subsidies, there are special let-outs for research and development.

We can all agree that innovation is a good thing and maybe it is worthy of a tax break. And it seems to be accepted that governments should spend our money encouraging us to do things we might not otherwise do, like riding a bike or eating healthy food. But there are also special tax breaks for the creators of video games and for filmmakers (more on these in the next chapter). Why films and video games should be deemed worthy of subsidy, while other successful industries like accountancy and building cars are not, is something of a mystery. Worse, as we'll see in the next chapter, these tax breaks have turned into a morass of fraud and avoidance.

So what is the logic of subsidising computer games but not factories? It isn't just about jobs. After all, plenty of UK workers are employed in the food-processing industry, but that does not get special treatment. Making movies is more glamorous than manufacturing baked beans, but that's not why we subsidise films. Rather, it's about mobility. There are lots of places where film producers can make movies and no particular reason why they should do it in the UK. Likewise, developing computer games is a job you can do anywhere. It makes no odds whether it is designed by a programmer working in Riga, Lisbon or Glasgow. A successful computer game developer can live where he or she likes, and pay taxes wherever that happens to be. Tax incentives exist to ensure computer games are developed in the UK and that all the royalties they generate from around the world are taxed here.

Intellectual property is of interest to tax authorities because of the way it can give rise to taxable royalties. Once BMW has assembled one of its Minis in Cowley, outside Oxford, and sold it, it has made all the money it ever will from that car. It is taxed on the profit and gets on with building another car. But successful research and development produces intellectual property that can continue to make money for years after it is finished. Ensuring that research and development is 'made' in the UK ensures all subsequent royalties from its exploitation are taxed here as well.

To further encourage intellectual property to stay in the UK, the government has also introduced a special system for taxing patent royalties. A patent is a kind of intellectual property, being the right of an inventor to benefit from his invention. Suppose you spent years working in your shed to come up with a new kind of stapler that doesn't jam if you try to staple more than ten sheets of paper. You want to sell your stapler without every other stationery company being able to copy it. To do this, you apply for a patent that means only you can exploit your invention for a set number of years. You can now either make the staplers yourself or sell your idea to a big company. It will pay you for the privilege to make staplers to your design, and these payments are called patent royalties. Obviously, these royalties are taxable so big companies, who hold most of the patents, find it worthwhile to move them to territories with low tax rates. To keep patents in the UK, where it can tax the resulting royalties, the British government has agreed that they will only be taxed at 10%.

The special tax breaks for research and development, patents and video games are all ways the government has come to terms with the knowledge economy. The stock-in-trade of the modern world are ideas – invisible and intangible. Even though you can't see them or touch them, they are immensely valuable and easy to transport across borders. To tax them, governments have to offer their owners a reason to stay put.

The trouble is, the more valuable a tax break, the bigger the temptation to abuse it. As we'll see in the next chapter, much avoidance is caused by government-mandated tax incentives being taken further than originally intended.

Taxes on financial transactions

In the wake of the financial crisis, banks have been subject to particular criticisms for their tax arrangements. One way that has been suggested to make them pay more is a financial transaction tax, often called the 'Robin Hood' tax. There are even pressure groups set up to push for such a levy. The EU has been considering a financial transaction tax for some time, although member states have found it hard to agree on the specifics. The UK is generally portrayed as being opposed, but in fact it has had such a tax for over a century – it's called stamp duty.

The idea of a financial transaction tax was originally put forward in the 1970s by the Nobel Prize-winning economist James Tobin, which is why it is sometimes called a Tobin Tax. He originally envisaged it as a levy charged every time one currency was exchanged for another. The idea has since been extended to other sorts of financial trading. The EU financial transaction tax would require a small amount to be paid over to the authorities each time a share or a bond is sold. The amount is a sliver of the price of the share or bond, somewhere between 0.1% and 1%. More ambitious versions of the tax would also tax exotic financial instruments called derivatives. Such is the enormous volume of trading in today's financial markets, even very low rates could lead to a substantial tax take.

Campaigners have dubbed the financial transaction tax the 'Robin Hood' tax because they imagine it would be paid by rich bankers and the proceeds given to the poor. James Tobin suggested the money raised should be given to developing nations. Certainly, a Robin Hood tax sounds good on social justice grounds. But sadly things are not that simple. The Second Golden Rule of tax will bite again: 'No matter what name is on the bill, all taxes are ultimately suffered by human beings.' Yes, a financial transaction tax would primarily be paid by banks, but they would pass the cost on to their customers. So a Tobin tax would not be borne by bankers. The people who would end up paying are bank customers like you and me, just like for every other tax.

James Tobin himself noted that if you set the rate high enough, you can prevent certain kinds of transactions by making them uneconomic. For example, Tobin actively wanted to discourage currency speculation. Today there are techniques, such as 'high-frequency trading', that have worried some people. Introducing a Tobin tax might stamp out high-frequency trading by making it uneconomic. It should certainly reduce the volume of financial transactions. When Sweden brought in a tax on selling bonds in 1989, with a rate of just 0.003%, the number of transactions fell by 85% in the first week. The tax ended up raising less than a tenth of what was expected and was scrapped in little more than a year.

In any case, economists can't make up their minds about whether financial speculation is a problem or not. Many recognise that it helps markets run more smoothly by ensuring that there are always plenty of buyers and sellers for shares, bonds and foreign currency. By discouraging speculation, transaction taxes make markets less liquid. The higher the taxes, the less efficient the market becomes (which, as we saw above, might mean we are storing up trouble for the UK property market where stamp duty land tax has become a very heavy transaction tax). Most governments prefer a healthy market that means they can collect more tax, rather than stopping people from speculating altogether.

So, a financial transaction tax with a low rate might be a good idea. You will recall the First Golden Rule of tax states that: 'Lots of small taxes together add up to make big tax bills.' A tax on financial transactions is a potential small tax that, if you set the rate at the right level, few people will notice. But you have to be careful. Bond traders don't have to operate in London, Paris or Frankfurt. They can trade from the beaches of the Caribbean or the bars of Hong Kong or their living rooms in Sydney. If the EU imposed a Tobin tax, financial traders might gradually drift away to more welcoming shores. It's likely that Germany and France would hang on to their domestic markets, but the effect on the City of London would be catastrophic. That's why the British government opposed the EU's plans for a financial transaction tax unless the rest of the world implements one too. This is sensible. Since a vast amount of business is done through London, the British Exchequer would be a major beneficiary of an international tax. But it would have to apply everywhere or any country that didn't implement it would quickly steal London's financial pre-eminence.

These objections meant that, even before Brexit, the UK was not part of the plans for an EU financial transaction tax. Even the countries that are interested in taking part are finding it very hard to agree exactly how it should work.

Luckily, there are some financial instruments that are not as mobile as bonds and derivatives. If you want to own shares in a listed UK company, almost the only place you can buy them is on the London Stock Exchange. Admittedly, there are special financial products called depositary receipts that can be traded in other countries and some companies, like Shell and HSBC, have dual listings in more than one country for historical reasons. But generally speaking, UK shares have to be bought and sold in London.

Since it is impractical to buy UK shares anywhere but in the UK, the government can tax share sales without worrying about all the business moving elsewhere. For many years, selling UK shares has been subject to a special levy called stamp duty reserve tax. This is collected automatically by the electronic settlement system of the London Stock Exchange. The rate is 0.5% of the price of the shares.

Although, nowadays, most shares are bought and sold electronically, it is still possible to hold shares via a certificate that requires the use of a paper stock transfer form to sell. In that case, you actually have to get the stock transfer form stamped by the taxman before you can be registered as the shares' new official owner.

Transaction taxes probably do make markets less efficient. But then, all taxes distort the economy in one way or another, and rarely in a positive way. It seems unlikely that a modest financial transaction tax would substantially increase turbulence in the markets (although, contrary to some commentators, it certainly wouldn't reduce it). Share prices in the UK, subject to a 0.5% impost on each sale, don't seem more volatile than shares in the USA, which are not.

This means there is hope for a slimmed down version of the European financial transaction tax if it is restricted to shares. Both France and Italy have jumped the EU gun and enacted their own version of the UK's stamp duty (Spain and Portugal have plans to do the same). Since quoted French and Italian shares are traded at the Bourse de Paris and Milan's Borsa Italiana respectively, these provide a captive market that governments can trim. Basically, other European countries are adopting the system that the UK has had for decades. When introducing new taxes, copying a successful model from elsewhere in the world is often a good idea. As we'll see in the next chapter, getting tax design wrong can cost governments a great deal of money.

5

Taxes evaded, avoided and reformed

Film finance: how governments encourage planning, avoidance and evasion

May 1997 seemed like the start of something special. Eighteen years of Conservative rule had come to an end. Tony Blair's Labour Party had seized power with a massive majority. Standing on the steps of the Royal Festival Hall, he promised a new dawn.

One group of people especially happy was Labour-supporting actors. Blair and his Chancellor, Gordon Brown, had made free use of film stars like Jeremy Irons and Alan Rickman to spread their political brand. Association with cinema made New Labour seem trendy and hip. This was the era of 'Cool Britannia'. So when Brown made it into government, he was ready to offer support to the British film industry. He did it by providing them with a substantial tax break.

The incentive worked as follows. Suppose you were a wealthy person who wanted to invest in the UK film industry. The government said that you could deduct the money that you invest from your total taxable income. For example, suppose Sir Simon Mogul makes £10,000,000 a year from his hedge fund. He decides to invest £500,000 in an arthouse film called *Naked Ramblers*. Sir Simon can then knock the £500,000 investment from his taxable income, meaning he only pays tax on £9.5 million instead of £10 million. With a 40% income tax rate, that is a cash saving of £200,000.

If the film makes money, Sir Simon will have to pay tax on his share of that income. But even if the film flops, he still gets to keep the £200,000 tax saving from his investment. Effectively, of the £500,000 investment Sir Simon makes, he pays £300,000 and tax-payers (that's you and me) pay £200,000. There was only one problem: few people want to risk their own money in the British film industry. After all, even with the tax break, Sir Simon still has to cough up £300,000. Thankfully, the City of London got to work and shortly came up with a solution. They turbo-charged New Labour's tax break with two further ingredients: leverage (which we met in Chapter 3) and defeasance. It is worth taking a moment to explain how these concepts provided steroids for the film industry.

Recall that Sir Simon has invested £500,000 of his own money in *Naked Ramblers*. The total production costs are more like £5 million, so Sir Simon borrows the remaining £4.5 million from the bank. The £500,000 of his own money is like the 10% deposit building societies require us to put down for a mortgage. But instead of buying a house, he has invested in a film. As we saw when we looked at the buy-to-let sector, borrowing money to invest, rather than just using your own, is called leverage. It is a way to get more bang for your buck. And thanks to the generosity of the government's tax break, Sir Simon can set the entire £5 million investment against his taxable income. With income tax at 40%, that is a tax saving of £2 million – four times the money he has put up himself. Of course, he does have to pay interest to the bank for the money he has borrowed and pay back the loan in due course. He will also have to pay tax on his share of any proceeds from the film. That is where the second ingredient, called defeasance, comes in.

Sir Simon doesn't want to risk his own money on a film. Nor does his bank. The people who are willing to take this risk are the film distributors who sell the rights to show the film in cinemas. If the film is a hit, the distributor makes money, and if it is a flop, they carry the can. Unlike Sir Simon and the bank, the distributors are professionals used to distinguishing between blockbusters and turkeys. Usually, the production company and the distributor will have already done a deal, back when the film was still just a glimmer in its scriptwriter's eye, to sell the distribution rights. In the case of *Naked Ramblers*, the distributor has already agreed to pay, you guessed it, £5 million.

That means Sir Simon can't lose: he has agreed to invest £5 million making a film that a distributor has already agreed to buy for the same amount. He gets his £5 million straight back. But because that money is treated as income, he would have to pay tax on it. No problem: the producer just pops the cash in the bank and arranges that Sir Simon is repaid over 15 years. The money is used to pay Sir Simon's tax bill as it falls due and repay his bank (an arrangement which is called a sale and leaseback). The end result is that Sir Simon gets a tax deduction of £5 million now and taxable income of the same amount spread over the next 15 years. He has no interest in the commercial success of *Naked Ramblers*.

This is a 'tax deferral' scheme. Sir Simon saves tax today that he has to pay some distant tomorrow. You'd have thought that HMRC might have had strenuous objections to all this. But it didn't. Perhaps under pressure from the government to make sure the tax break for films wasn't a damp squib, they published a statement of practice that said the leverage and defeasance scheme was legit. All of a sudden, there was an officially sanctioned way to delay your tax bills by up to 15 years.

Everyone thought this was splendid. Accountants started to corral together wealthy people to invest in the scheme and defer their taxes. Banks lent out billions with no chance of a default. Investors showered film production companies with cash. Lots of films were made in the UK, including James Bond adventures, Steven Spielberg productions and Disney fairy tales. The actors who'd supported Labour were happy and the government was happy. I suppose that if this book were scurrilous, I might dwell on the unparalleled awfulness of some of the films financed by the scheme. A few were not released for years afterwards. As far as I know, some of them still haven't been. This is probably for the best.

With so much money being poured into film production by wealthy investors, it wasn't long before there weren't enough films to go around. Television production companies piled into the bonanza. First of all it was costume dramas, which at least had the production values of a real movie. But fairly soon any old TV programme was being used, including soap operas. *Coronation Street*, *Holby City* and *Eastenders* all became beneficiaries of a tax scheme intended for the British film industry. And all this was being done with the explicit connivance of the tax authority itself. It couldn't last. In 2002, Gordon Brown banned television shows from benefiting. In 2006, the scheme was cancelled altogether.

As we saw in Chapter 4, the official reason for providing tax breaks to the British film industry is that a film is a kind of intellectual property. Films and television shows can be made in lots of places, all of which are keen to attract them. One reason the celebrated series *Breaking Bad* was set in Albuquerque was the generous tax subsidy that the US State of New Mexico was willing to offer the production company. So a good rationale for subsidising film production is that everyone else is doing it. And, because the French insisted, there is a special carve out from the EU's anti-subsidies rules for the creative sector.

There is no doubt that the tax break introduced in 1997 caused a great deal of money to be invested in British film production, some of which would not have otherwise been available. But the scheme also cost taxpayers (again, that's you and me) a great deal of money. Many of the good films that the scheme supported would have been made in the UK in any case. So it is impossible to say whether the Labour Party's desire to reward its celebrity supporters (or support the British film industry, depending on your point of view) was of a net benefit to the UK.

Under a revised scheme introduced on 1 January 2007, the film production companies are now awarded the tax break rather than the rich investors. Giving the tax relief to the people making the film is sensible because they are the ones who are at risk if it is a flop. That didn't stop tax planners from attempting to take advantage of the new rules. Investors still tried to gain access to the tax break using elaborate structures to make it look like they were in the movie business without having to get their hands dirty making films. This time, HMRC was not so supportive. It went to court and has so far won several high-profile cases. The judges decided that the investors were not trading as film producers and so were not entitled to the tax breaks that they were expecting. Other tax planners have tried to exploit the incentives for developing vaccines without going near a petri dish and for computer games without handling a joystick. Again, HMRC is winning the subsequent court battles. On the evidence so far, it looks like current rules leak a lot less than the old system. But it is impossible to work out whether the cost to the taxpayer of providing even the revised tax incentives is really worth the benefit of more films and computer games being made in the UK.

For those without access to clever advisors to help them exploit loopholes in the film finance rules, there is always outright fraud to fall back on. That was the plan of a gang led by an Irish actress called Aoife Madden. While big production companies can only deduct the cost of the film from their taxable profits, small companies can get the cash equivalent of the tax benefit from producing a film while they are still making it. HMRC just send them a cheque. So, the gang pretended they were making a film with a star-studded cast and a budget of £19 million. They sent fake paperwork into HMRC and received cheques for over £2 million by return. For good measure, they also sent in dodgy VAT returns and reclaimed VAT they had not suffered.

It took a while, but eventually HMRC cottoned on to what was happening. It asked to see some evidence that the film was taking shape, but only received a grainy home video. With the noose closing, the gang realised that they would have to do better than that. The obvious answer was to produce a real film. They were claiming tax refunds on the basis that their film had a budget of £19 million, so if they could pull one together for a £100,000 or so and throw HMRC off their scent, they'd still be quids in. Unfortunately, making a film was way beyond the abilities of a gang of fraudsters, so they needed to recruit a legitimate producer.

The resulting film was called, appropriately enough, *Landscape of Lies*. It is about an Iraq War veteran returning to London and being sucked into the criminal underworld. Instead of the big-name stars the gang had originally promised HMRC they would use, *Landscape of Lies* features a cast of talented unknowns. It is, by all accounts, pretty good. It has won an award and its producer had hoped for a cinema release.

Whatever the quality of the result, HMRC was not fooled. The gang found themselves on trial for fraud and tax evasion at South-wark Crown Court in London where they were convicted and sentenced to up to six and a half years in prison. Media coverage of the trial probably did the film *Landscape of Lies* no harm. Although seeing all its backers jailed does stretch the old adage that there is no such thing as bad publicity.

The whole film finance fiasco shows the danger of offering tax incentives to favoured causes. The government wanted to encourage film production and did so by reducing the risks of investing in a film. When it became clear that the risks could be reduced to nothing, money piled in. This didn't just cost the Exchequer more money than it had bargained for, it also created economic distortions. Yes, money was being invested in films and TV, just as the government wanted, but this was not because it was a good investment. People were only doing it for the tax benefit. As a result, more deserving investments that might have helped the economy grow were crowded out. I wouldn't say that it is always a bad idea to use the tax system to encourage certain kinds of behaviour, but it does always have unintended consequences.

Taxation has its own irregular verb form: I plan; you avoid; he evades. The film finance tax break can help us understand these often-confused terms: planning, avoidance and evasion. The words have precise meanings among tax professionals, but they are readily conflated by the media and politicians.

When the incentive for films was first introduced in 1997, taking advantage of it was doing what the government wanted. Even the defeasance structure was officially approved by the taxman. This made it legitimate tax planning. Full disclosure: I worked on a lot of these kind of deals in the period up to 2003. Then, in 2006, the government changed its policy and said that henceforth, only the people actually making the film should get the benefits. Attempts to use elaborate schemes to let sleeping partners enjoy the incentive after this change in policy were tax avoidance. That meant the schemes were attempts to stay within the letter of the law, but outside the policy that the law was supposed to implement. As we've seen, the courts are currently examining these avoidance schemes and concluding that many of them don't work.

Finally, the gang who made *Landscape of Lies* were fraudsters. What they were doing was blatantly illegal. It meant pulling the wool over the tax authority's eyes: that was clearly tax evasion. But evasion is more widespread and rarely involves criminal gangs with elaborate conspiracies. Far from it: tax evasion is dead easy.

Let's look at each of evasion, avoidance and planning in more detail.

Tax evasion

If you deliberately 'forget' to tell the taxman about the £1,500 you received for helping out your neighbour with their home improvements, you are committing a crime. If you negotiate a lower price from the electrician for paying him in cash, on the understanding that it helps him reduce his tax bill, you are facilitating evasion. Simply using cash rather than a bank transfer is not untoward. However, it crosses a line to agree a price reduction where this represents your share of the benefit from a tradesman being able to keep his earnings out of the tax net.

When the Treasury minister David Gauke pointed all this out in 2012, the media rounded on him for turning everyone into criminals. Labour's Ed Balls said the same thing in 2015, calling for people who pay cash-in-hand to ask for a receipt. Again, he was castigated, especially when it was found that he did not always practise what he preached. People just don't like it when their behaviour is questioned. After all, when it comes to cash-in-hand, 'everyone does it'.

Let's take a closer look at what tax evasion involves and the amount of money the government loses as a result.

For rich individuals, the paradigmatic example of evasion is having a bank account in a secretive country like Switzerland or Liechtenstein. If you live in the UK, you must pay income tax on the interest you earn offshore. If you fail to declare that income, you are a tax evader. However, hiding money from the taxman is becoming progressively more difficult.

For many years, Switzerland refused to divulge who had accounts at its banks. It claimed that the responsibility for declaring income was with individual taxpayers. However, in the last couple of years, many countries have entered into information sharing agreements so that, for instance, HMRC can soon ask for the names of all UK citizens with Swiss bank accounts. The USA has gone even further. Under the Foreign Account Tax Compliance Act (FATCA for short), no international bank or fund manager can do business in the USA without disclosing all the US citizens who hold accounts with it. Figuring out who all their clients are and where they come from is a massive burden on the banks, which their customers will end up paying for. As one senior banker explained to me, it's the equivalent of having to find out if everyone you meet is an American and to report them to the US government if they are. Of course, FATCA is a godsend for the accountants and consultants who end up doing all the work. But, after years of refusing to disclose anything, banks can't be surprised that governments have lost patience.

The increased transparency of the international banking system has made concealing money more difficult for terrorists and drug dealers as well as for run-of-the-mill tax evaders. They might quibble about the bureaucracy involved, but most banks now accept that they must be good corporate citizens. Nonetheless, there is still a long way to go to defeat evasion. Determined evaders can conceal their assets in less salubrious parts of the world. But that might not be very advisable. Depositors at banks in Cyprus lost large amounts when the country's financial system collapsed in 2013. Keeping your money safe should be a higher priority than keeping it out of sight.

If individuals are determined not to pay UK tax, they can leave the country and move somewhere else. When you live in a haven, you are legitimately subject to its low rates of tax. The most famous such bolthole is Monaco, the small principality on the French Riviera, home to Formula One drivers and many of the super rich. International sports stars spend much of their lives living out of a suitcase making it easy for them to choose a convenient territory, like Monaco, in which to be officially resident. That said, my one visit to Monaco (for a tax conference, naturally) convinced me that the principality is as close to purgatory as you will find this side of the grave. Another popular tax haven is Jersey. This is nice enough if you like peace and quiet. But a colleague who briefly had to live there for professional reasons found it was no place to be young and hip. She couldn't wait to leave.

It's not just the rich who evade taxes. Traders taking cash-in-hand, which they 'forget' to include in their tax calculations, have always been a problem. Cash payments certainly won't appear on an evader's VAT returns either. We saw in Chapter 1 how the PAYE system means most people never write a cheque to HMRC. The self-employed have to pay their taxes directly. It is hardly surprising that many resent having to pay tax on profits that they have worked so hard for. Keeping a little bit of cash out of the equation can be a difficult temptation to resist.

Added to this, smugglers circumvent the UK's high excise duties on cigarettes and spirits simply by buying them elsewhere in the European Union to sell them back at home. Finally, there are criminal gangs who deliberately defraud the taxman through elaborate scams like the one we saw earlier on film finance.

No one really knows how big the problem of the black market is. HMRC estimates that tax evasion and the hidden economy cost the government £16 billion a year. That's a lot. The missing money has to be raised by increasing taxes on the rest of us. Nonetheless, HMRC tends to take a softly-softly approach to tax evasion. Criminal prosecutions are expensive and the burden of proof is high. Juries are not always ready to convict evaders for the crime of hanging onto their own money, even if they are doing it illegally. Over the years, the Revenue has lost some high profile cases, such as against the football manager Harry Redknapp in 2012 and entertainer Ken Dodd in 1990. Both were found not guilty. Dodd's evidence from the witness box did an excellent job of convincing the jury that he was a naïf when it came to money. As his barrister, the late George Carman QC, told the jury, 'Some accountants are comedians, but comedians are never accountants.' Dodd also made the court laugh. HMRC alleged he kept his wealth in cash to evade tax, but Dodd said it was just convenient. When the judge asked him 'What does £100,000 in a suitcase feel like?' the comedian replied: 'The notes are very light m'Lud.'

Rather than risk embarrassing defeats, HMRC will commonly offer amnesties coupled with financial penalties. For instance, when the UK and Swiss governments signed an information-sharing agreement in 2012, HMRC gave anyone who had an undeclared Swiss bank account the chance to come clean. By paying all the back taxes they owe, together with the same amount again for good measure, evaders can wipe the slate clean without risking a criminal record.

This approach recovered £1.5 billion in back taxes and fines during 2013. We can't close down all the tax havens, but we can force people who want to hide their money to do so in places where it is not as safe as a vault in Zurich. In a way, HMRC is like the Spanish Inquisition. Both institutions, despite their fearsome reputations, don't want to create martyrs by handing people over to the secular arm (or the crown prosecution service, in the case of the taxman). They would rather use gentler ways to persuade offenders of the error of their ways, and collect a good deal of extra money into the bargain.

Tax avoidance and the general anti-abuse rule

It is a settled principle that you don't have to pay more tax than the law demands. All debates on avoidance, abuse and planning boil down to asking what it is that the rules require. For many tax practitioners, the divide between acceptable planning and unacceptable abuse can be stated as follows: if you are going to do something anyway, such as buy a company or machine, lend money or restructure your business, you should be allowed to do it in a way that produces the most tax efficient outcome. But if you are doing something that you would not be doing otherwise purely to reduce your tax bill, then that is more likely to be abusive.

That leaves open what to do about legal loopholes. If the law is deficient in some way, so it doesn't do what it says on the tin, can a taxpayer take advantage of this? For a long time, the answer was yes, they can. This was especially the case when two complicated bits of tax legislation combined to give a strange result that Parliament could never have envisaged, even if that was because the drafter of the law never considered the situation in question. Where tax schemes have succeeded in the courts in recent years, this is usually why. A clever lawyer or accountant has realised that two bits of the tax code tell them to do different things. Combine both into a transaction and interesting effects can result. Since both bits of legislation are doing what they are supposed to do, and the tax advantage arises only from their interaction, the courts cannot do much about it (although they do usually try very hard to find a way around the problem). As one judge recently put it, there will be 'cases which will inevitably occur from time to time in a tax system as complicated as ours [where] a well advised taxpayer has been able to take advantage of an unintended gap left by the interaction between two different sets of statutory provisions'.

The UK tax avoidance industry was born following the Second World War, which, as we saw in Chapter 1, was an era of astronomically high personal tax rates. With income tax reaching a peak 98% in the 1970s, it was hardly surprising that sheltering earnings from tax was a popular activity. These very high tax rates were an inheritance from the war, when people accepted that the country needed every penny it could lay its hands on to defeat Hitler. But after the conflict, personal taxes stayed high whether the government was Conservative or Labour. This led to an erosion of the legitimacy of the tax system. Success was something that was penalised by the state. Conversely, accountants had little trouble finding loopholes in the UK's antiquated tax code. For a start, as we saw in Chapter 3, there was no capital gains tax until 1965. But most importantly, there was a recognition by the courts that when tax rates were so high, people were perfectly entitled to use any legal means to hang on to their own money.

In several famous cases, judges had defended the right of taxpayers to arrange their affairs to minimise their tax bill. As the Lord President of the Council put it in 1929: 'No man in this country is under the smallest obligation, moral or other, so to arrange his legal relations to his business or to his property as to enable the Inland Revenue to put the largest possible shovel in his stores.' This principle was supported in the House of Lords in 1935 in a famous case over how the Duke of Westminster remunerated his staff. 'Every man,' their Lordships proclaimed, 'is entitled, if he can, to order his affairs so that the tax attaching . . . is less than it otherwise would be.'

The so-called Duke of Westminster principle remained a precedent for decades. Taxpayers whose accountants had contrived the most artificial schemes found that they could keep a hold of more of their money. Governments responded with anti-avoidance laws, like the provisions to stop bond washing that we saw in Chapter 3. The fossilised remains of these rules are still buried in the tax code ensuring that the law is a little bit more prolix than it needs to be.

This was also the era of the tax exile. For British film stars and pop groups, whose earnings largely arose abroad, it made little sense to live in the UK. Scientists and businessmen also saw the attractions of moving overseas, in a flow of talent out of the country that came to be called the brain drain. For those who were left behind, it became acceptable for companies to pay their employees in ways that didn't attract tax. Fat expense accounts and company cars were the order of the day. The television presenter Sir David Frost used an elaborate scheme to ensure that the money he was making in the USA from interviewing disgraced ex-President Richard Nixon was not taxed in the UK where he lived. The Inland Revenue took Frost to court, but it lost all the way up to the House of Lords. Frost's successful tax planning attracted nothing like the opprobrium that today's celebrities endure when their activities are revealed.

For politicians, this was all very frustrating. As the Labour Chancellor of the Exchequer, later Prime Minister, Jim Callaghan, said in the 1960s, 'There are plenty of people in the City today who know their way round the [tax] code like many of my constituents know their way to Cardiff docks, or to the steel works. They know how to use the existing tax code and they have found means of using it.' Since accountants knew the tax code better than either the politicians or tax inspectors, they had little trouble running rings around the authorities.

A changing climate

Then, in May 1979, uttering the prayer of St Francis of Assisi, Margaret Thatcher entered 10 Downing Street. Her Chancellor, Geoffrey Howe, immediately cut the top rate of income tax to 60%. The reduction of tax rates from 83% reduced the incentive to evade or avoid taxes. But more significantly, it changed the moral calculus of taxation. When the government is trying to take almost every extra penny you earn, no one can blame you for wanting to keep back as much for yourself as you can. Tax has to be fair and the rates between the Second World War and 1979 manifestly were not. Judges, who paid a few bob in tax themselves, applied the law to tax schemes but didn't go any further. There was little public condemnation of tax avoidance.

Mrs Thatcher changed that, albeit indirectly. She wanted people who worked hard to get on. She felt they had a right to keep more of what they earned. But conversely, people had to pay their dues. Her governments enacted tough anti-avoidance rules against companies and individuals who kept their money in tax havens. Judges also began to look upon elaborate avoidance schemes less sympathetically.

As we've seen, lawyers and accountants had previously been able to rely on the courts to interpret tax rules literally. This made avoidance schemes easy to dream up. Tax experts simply had to invent a situation that the drafters of the law had never imagined. These situations rarely had much commercial substance. Money moved in a circle, so there wasn't any chance of a real profit or loss. But as the money completed its circuit, it changed its nature for tax purposes, generating reliefs and losses when no real expenditure had been incurred.

The accountants of a certain landowner, Robert Ramsay, advised him to use such a scheme. He was selling some land and had to pay a large amount of capital gains tax on the sale. So his advisors suggested a transaction whereby he generated an artificial capital loss to set against his gain. Given the egregious nature of these arrangements, the taxman had no hesitation taking Mr Ramsay to court. As the case wended its way up the chain to the Court of Appeal, the various judges who heard it decided this particular scheme probably didn't work. But the taxman wanted to achieve something more. When the case finally reached the House of Lords in 1981, the Inland Revenue asked the law lords to rule that this sort of wholly unrealistic and non-commercial transaction should fail on principle.

By then, as we've seen, the ethical case against tax avoidance had been strengthened by Margaret Thatcher's cuts in the top rates of income tax. But the Inland Revenue had another thing going for them. The lead law lord hearing the case was Richard Wilberforce, great-great-grandson of the abolitionist William Wilberforce. He was a man who believed in common sense and the supremacy of Parliament. He wasn't much taken by legal chicanery. So when the case of *Ramsay v Commissioners of the Inland Revenue* came before him, he was ready to reach a radical decision. He also managed to carry with him the other four law lords hearing the case.

Lord Wilberforce decided that it was no longer acceptable to just interpret the letter of the law. Judges should decide tax cases based on the facts on the ground rather than their legal form. The transactions from which Mr Ramsay had generated his capital loss had no economic reality: the money ended up where it started. So under Lord Wilberforce's newly-minted 'Ramsay principle', the transaction wasn't to have any tax effect either. Since there had been no real transaction, Mr Ramsay was not allowed to have the capital loss his planning was supposed to generate. His accountants' avoidance scheme had no effect.

Although this wasn't the end of highly contrived tax schemes, it did make them more difficult. The situation wasn't helped by disagreements among judges and lawyers about what the Ramsay principle truly meant. The Inland Revenue wanted to treat it as a universal acid that could dissolve any tax avoidance on touch. Taxpayers, unsurprisingly, believed that only completely artificial arrangements should be affected.

Banks, who move money around in the ordinary course of their business were least disadvantaged by the Ramsay principle. They could almost always find a commercial transaction onto which they could hook a tax scheme. Given how complicated international finance was in any case, it was easier for banks to claim that contrived schemes were nothing out of the ordinary. In the 1990s, investment banks set up special units that specialised in so-called 'structured finance'. This meant developing ways to lend and borrow money in a tax-efficient way. Members of these teams had brains the size of planets and compensation packages to match. Then, in 2008, came the financial crisis and suddenly the banks were under intense public scrutiny. Worse, they had no money. There was little point in them avoiding corporation tax if a lack of profits meant they weren't paying it anyway. It is safe to say there are far fewer bankers working in structured finance today than there were a few years ago.

Avoiding income tax

Public concern about tax avoidance is not restricted to banks. You might remember the case of Jimmy Carr, a TV comedian, who was avoiding a great deal of tax on his considerable income. He did this by arranging that he was lent money instead of being paid it. His earnings were paid to a company in Jersey, which wasn't subject to any tax. The company lent him the money interest free to spend as he pleased. The law treats this interest-free loan as a taxable benefit. But the point was, he only paid tax on what the interest on the loan should have been. Even though he was never going to repay the debt, the gross amount wasn't treated as taxable income. The net result was an effective income tax rate of about 1% instead of 40% or 50%. When Carr's involvement in the scheme was leaked to the press, public pressure quickly led to him withdrawing.

Jimmy Carr found the whole affair acutely embarrassing, but escaped largely unscathed, except for a bigger tax bill. The consequences of tax avoidance are not always so mild. Until 2011, Glasgow Rangers had been the premier club of Scottish football. Together with Celtic, they formed the Old Firm, who shared the league title between them almost every year (the only exception anyone can remember was when Alex Ferguson's Aberdeen were champions in the 1980s). In recent years, the success of Celtic meant that Rangers had to lure ever more expensive foreign players to Glasgow. These footballers didn't really care about UK taxes. They were simply interested in their net pay, or the amount that ends up in their pockets.

Because the players were guaranteed their take-home pay no matter what tax had to be paid, it was the football clubs that picked up the tax bill. This was an invitation for the clubs to avoid taxes on players' salaries. It was risky because if the schemes went wrong, the club and not the player had to make good the extra tax. Arsenal was especially adroit at these deals. When the courts examined their contract with the Dutch star Dennis Bergkamp, they found it stacked up. HMRC lost the case, but could change the law. So, when Rangers tried the technique of lending cash to their players that would never be paid back, HMRC was confident of victory. In fact, it was so confident that it pushed Rangers into bankruptcy over unpaid tax bills. The club had to ply its trade on the muddy pitches of the lower leagues until 2016 and Celtic had no rival for the title. You might say that tax avoidance has made Scottish football even less of a contest than it was before.

Nonetheless, when the Rangers case came before a tax tribunal in 2012, HMRC contrived to lose. This surprised many tax practitioners. Of the three judges in the case, two sided with Rangers and one with HMRC. Reading the decision, I think the minority report certainly looks the better argued. HMRC then launched an appeal and managed to lose again, before finally winning in Scotland's highest court. The case is now due to be heard at the Supreme Court in London and the tax world is waiting for the final score with baited breath.

Despite occasional reverses for the taxman, the lesson from the cases of Jimmy Carr and Glasgow Rangers is clear: taking part in these contrived schemes to avoid tax is extremely risky. It is not just the financial costs: the damage to an avoider's reputation can be just as great.

Sadly, the taxman has not always helped the moral case against using loopholes in the law. HMRC can be happy to exploit them itself when naive taxpayers get caught out by the ridiculous complexity of our tax code. If the taxman is willing to extract windfalls from wholly innocent taxpayers, he can hardly complain when better-advised avoiders turn the system to their advantage. In a recent case, a certain Joost Lobler managed to cash out his life insurance policies in the wrong order and was hit by a wholly unwarranted tax bill for £300,000. The sensible thing for HMRC to have done would be to accept that Mr Lobler had made an honest mistake and let him correct it. Instead, they took him to court. The initial judge was extremely sympathetic but still ordered him to cough up. Luckily a more senior judge saw sense and ordered HMRC to drop its claim. If tax authorities want the big banks and rich individuals to obey the spirit as well as the letter of the law, they really need to do the same thing when dealing with other taxpayers. Instead, in the Lobler case, HMRC acted very poorly.

The new fight against aggressive avoidance

In the aftermath of the financial crisis, the UK found itself with a budget deficit of over £150 billion. The incoming Coalition government immediately raised taxes and started to cut public expenditure. But there was another element to its tax policy that has been far less controversial: the Coalition was tougher on tax avoidance than any previous government in history, and the current Conservative government has been continuing the fight.

We looked at the international base erosion and profit shifting agenda instigated by David Cameron against avoidance by multinational companies in the last chapter. For income tax avoidance, the government has introduced policies that can, in combination, only be described as draconian. There are three elements to this. The first was a new general anti-abuse rule. The aim of the rule is to prevent contrived schemes from taking advantage of loopholes and gaps in the law. As we have seen, the rules are so complicated that cunning advisors have been able to find ways of using them to avoid taxes for many years. Where specific anti-avoidance provisions are introduced, even these can be subverted and turned to taxpayers' advantage. The general anti-abuse rule is supposed to short-circuit that process. Where taxpayers do something contrived purely to avoid tax, then the anti-abuse rule can prevent the arrangement from working. Unlike previous anti-avoidance rules, it has general applicability and does not specify the particular kind of avoidance it is aimed at. This means that it acts as a kind of legislative Polyfilla, to plug the loopholes in the legislation so that they can no longer be used to defeat the purpose of the law. The anti-abuse rule is not intended to prevent taxpayers planning their affairs tax-efficiently, but just to stop the worst kinds of aggressive tax avoidance. As such, Labour MP Shabana Mahmood, among others, has complained that it lacks teeth. Nonetheless, this is the first overarching defence against exploiting loopholes that the UK has ever had.

A second element of the government's fight against tax avoidance has been forcing those involved in aggressive schemes to pay what they owe before the courts have finally decided their case. Tax cases can drag on for years as they become subject to appeals higher up the chain, potentially all the way to the Supreme Court. In all that time, there is no requirement to pay any tax. So now, under a new rule, the government hangs onto the money while the courts are ruminating over their decisions. The avoider will only get paid back if he ends up winning the case, which looks increasingly unlikely as judges continue to take a dim view of aggressive tax schemes.

The final step taken by the government was the most drastic of all. For the small minority who simply refuse to pay up, HMRC will soon be able to extract the cash owed directly from the miscreants' bank accounts. Together these three measures add up to a package that should make tax avoiders think twice.

Tax planning

As we've seen, it is supposed to be a principle of the UK tax system that we don't have to pay more than the law demands. In theory, that means that tax planning is still acceptable. If avoidance and planning are both legal, how can we tell one from the other? To add to the confusion, public perception of tax planning is rapidly changing. Lots of techniques, which were considered benign planning when I started my career 20 years ago, are now frowned upon. Some of the change is a function of activists protesting against tax avoidance. I think it is also the gradual development of a new philosophy: get tax rates as low as possible and make sure everyone pays. With corporation tax cut to just 20% and falling, combined with measures like the new diverted profits tax, we are seeing this philosophy implemented for business tax. Abolishing tax incentives and planning opportunities while cutting overall tax rates is certainly a good idea. But, as we will see, tax reform is politically challenging to pull off.

In this book, we've looked at many officially sanctioned tax-reduction schemes to make us behave in the way the government wants us to. An obvious example is the ISA or individual savings account, which, as we've already seen, allows us to make tax-free investments, subject to the maximum of £15,240 a year. There are also tax breaks for activities that range from charitable giving to riding a bicycle. Whether these incentives are a good idea is a moot point. Are you really going to start cycling to work to save a bit of tax? Most people won't. Even if a few do, people who cycle anyway get the lion's share of the benefit. It's debatable whether this is an efficient use of public money. A few years ago, employers were allowed to give all their staff a computer under Gordon Brown's Home Computer Initiative. I was thrilled. I never say no to a new computer. But precisely why the government felt the need to subsidise equipment that I used mainly for playing video games like *Half-Life* and *Civilization* was mysterious. Unfortunately, once they exist, trying to sweep away these incentives is not easy. If the government decided, reasonably enough, that the bicycle subsidy wasn't doing much good, the howls of outrage from the green lobby and aggrieved cyclists would be deafening. Luckily, in 2006, Gordon Brown did manage to ditch his tax-free computers without too many grumbles.

One aspect of the UK tax system that has upset plenty of people is the treatment of 'non-doms'. A non-dom is someone who is not 'domiciled' in the UK. Under tax law, your domicile is your home country even if you now permanently live somewhere else. Being a non-dom is similar to being an expatriate – someone who has left his or her fatherland. One great attraction of the UK for rich immigrants is that people who are not domiciled here only have to pay tax on money that they bring into the country. They can keep the rest of it locked up in Swiss bank accounts without bothering HMRC. Instead, the non-doms pay an annual fee of up to £90,000 a year (plus normal tax on any money they earn or bring into the UK).

Tax is not the only thing that the super rich consider when deciding where to live. A supply of fine restaurants, designer clothing shops and somewhere to moor the yacht are relevant. So is a good cultural scene and luxury houses. All of which means that many tax exiles wind up in the UK and especially in London.

There has been a good deal of controversy over non-doms' tax status in the UK. Many people believe that if they live in the UK, non-doms should pay the same taxes as everyone else. I am sure the government would love it if they could tax the enormous wealth of some of these people. But it also recognises that they are uniquely mobile. By living in the UK, they have already made a choice to leave their homeland and they could just as well move somewhere else. No one doubts that they benefit the UK economy, through their skills and by spending their money. They also bankroll a considerable part of football's Premier League. Nonetheless, their special tax status is unfair. Until they have been resident in the UK for 15 years, they get all the advantages of living in the UK without the tax disadvantages of being domiciled here.

It's up to governments to balance fairness with other benefits, and successive Chancellors of the Exchequer have decided to tolerate the infelicity of the non-doms' tax status. Their economic benefits are simply too great. It isn't equitable. But neither is it a case of politicians doing favours for their friends (as we sometimes hear insinuated). In a globalised world, governments have to look at the big picture and act in the national interest. And if that sometimes means they offer special deals to people whose presence benefits the country, that is what they must do, even if it sticks in the craw.

The government's approach to non-doms' taxation over the last decade has been to gradually ratchet up the amount of tax they have to pay. At each stage, it can measure the revenues it receives against any downside from non-doms taking flight. This pragmatic approach gives us the best of both worlds, providing non-doms with a reason to stay in the UK while also taxing them as much as practicably possible.

For the rest of us, we can save tax by using ISAs and contributing into pension plans, but only to the extent that we have spare cash to do so. We've already seen that if you are rich, opportunities for tax planning are a great deal more lucrative. What, if anything, should the government be doing about the fundamental unfairness of much of its revenue-raising machine, as well as its tremendous complexity? I've spent this book explaining how the tax system works. In the last section, let me indulge in making a few suggestions on how to improve it.

Tax reform

Ask almost anyone whether he or she, personally, pays enough tax and you'll be answered with a resounding 'yes'. In fact, most of us think we pay too much. But people also believe that governments should spend more money on health, education and other public services. That's why, in 2016, the British government ran a deficit, the difference between what it spends and what it gathers in taxes, of £69 billion.

So, if more taxes are required, who should pay them? To many people, the answer is simple: not them, someone else. Or, more specifically, the rich and multinational companies. But, as we've already seen, matters are not that simple. We tax high earners as much as we can and taxing companies is a bad idea economically. Of late, we've also heard a lot about tax avoiders paying their fair share and cracking down on tax evasion. The government is taking stringent action in this area as well, but the money raised won't be enough to close the deficit. Perhaps more radical change is needed.

To reiterate what I noted earlier, the problem with tax reform is that there are always winners and losers. The winners are quietly happy. The losers phone their lobbyists and opposition politicians stir the pot. There was an outcry in the newspapers about the injustice of slapping VAT on Cornish pasties and domestic fuel. Usually the government responds with a string of concessions or exemptions to compensate the losers. The law ends up more muddled than it started. That means it is often only possible to reform and simplify taxes in an environment when they are generally being cut. Everyone is winning, but some people are winning more than others. That keeps the moans to a minimum. But it also means that, with a huge budget deficit for the government to clear, we're unlikely to see meaningful tax simplification any time soon. On the contrary, in recent years the system has been getting ever more convoluted. Nevertheless, improvements to the tax system are possible; they just tend to be small and incremental.

With that in mind, I've set out below a short list of proposed tax reforms to make the system fairer and more efficient. They are listed in order of political realism. The first couple of suggestions could be implemented without too much fuss, while the latter ideas would require a brave Chancellor of the Exchequer to push them through.

1. Stop cutting income tax and start cutting national insurance

The Coalition government raised the income tax personal allowance over the life of the last Parliament, and the Conservatives intend to keep doing the same through the current one. The Labour Party want to reintroduce a 10p starting rate for income tax. They are all pursuing the wrong policy. Cutting income tax benefits everyone, including wealthy people who can live off their savings. In contrast, we've seen how national insurance, which is not affected by these cuts, is a tax only paid by those in work, whether they are employed or self-employed. This means that the tax system has a built in bias against people who are productive.

The government should stop cutting income tax or raising the personal allowance. Instead, it should increase the national insurance threshold and cut the rate of NICs. This would mean poorer workers kept more of their pay, helping them to escape from the poverty trap. It would be of no advantage to people who don't work.

2. Start the 45% tax rate at £100,000 instead of £150,000

As we saw in Chapter 1, the marginal rate of income tax increases from 40% to 60% at £100,000, currently drops back to 40% at £122,000 and then increases to 45% at £150,000. High marginal rates are economically damaging, but cutting the top rate from 45% would be politically inadvisable. Instead, we should simplify the regime by increasing the income tax rate from 40% to 45% for all income of £100,000 and over, while getting rid of the excessive 60% rate.

3. Tax companies according to their accounting profits

Corporation tax is charged on a company's taxable profits rather than the profits it shows in its accounts. As I mentioned in Chapter 4, this provides a great deal of work for accountants who get paid to make all the amendments to accounting profits to get taxable profits. Special tax rules also provide opportunities for avoidance. Companies should just be taxed on their bottom lines, without any tax adjustments. That means getting rid of tax incentives as well, since there is precious little evidence that they are an efficient way of altering corporate behaviour. Abolishing capital allowances, research and development incentives, the patent box and other distortions would simplify the system and ensure companies made decisions for commercial reasons rather than to chase tax breaks.

4.   Expand the scope of VAT

We've seen that there are good political reasons why VAT on books and children's clothes is 0%. Economically, this is nonsensical. Still, I am not going to suggest any Chancellor of the Exchequer should be so foolhardy as to do anything about it. However, extending the scope of VAT to include processed foods like ready meals, all forms of biscuits and snacks, breakfast cereals and condiments would raise a lot of money while potentially helping us to eat more healthily. The proposed levy on sugary soft drinks to be introduced in 2018 is a step in this direction, although it would be simpler just to increase the rate of VAT on fizzy drinks and squash. The flip side of my suggestion is it would make VAT even more complicated than it already is. Perhaps all the tax consultants out of work due to my previous idea to simplify corporation tax could retrain in indirect taxes like VAT.

5.   Introduce a minimum income tax rate for the wealthy while abolishing most income tax anti-avoidance rules and incentives

We saw in Chapter 3 how easy it is for people with money in the bank to reduce their income tax bills. And if the wealthy don't work, they don't have to pay national insurance either. I would set a minimum income tax rate of at least 30% on gross income and capital gains from any source except for employment or self-employment. The 30% rate would apply before any allowances for losses (including capital losses), special tax incentives, anti-avoidance rules or any other complications. Although a 30% rate would be lower than the headline rate, it would increase the amount people had to pay because they wouldn't be able to game the system. Tax avoidance for the wealthy would be a waste of time.

Conclusion: the Three Golden Rules of tax

Taxation is political. We all have our own ideas about how the system functions and how it should change. My aim in this book is not to resolve those debates. Instead, I want to show the way tax affects ordinary people and provide some context to the stories about avoidance we read in the newspapers. And I've tried to explain why the tax system works the way it does. Let's finish up by reminding ourselves of the Three Golden Rules of tax and by seeing how they apply to Britain's newest tax, the soft drinks industry levy or 'sugar tax'.

The First Golden Rule: Lots of small taxes together add up to make big tax bills

In Chapter 1, we saw that national insurance contributions are kept separate from income tax. There is no earthly reason for this except the government doesn't want to admit that, once you factor in NICs, the basic rate of income tax is effectively 32% for people in work, not the headline rate of 20%. We also have taxes on insurance premiums, airline seats, televisions, legacies and capital gains. There are taxes on selling shares and selling houses. We pay a tax for our cars and lots of tax when we fill them with petrol. If we smoke, we're taxed. If we drink, we're taxed. We pay tax on our houses and offices. Not all taxes raise much money. Aggregates levy brings in £355 million; landfill tax £919 million and cider duty just £296 million. But a billion here and a billion there and soon you are talking about real money, as the US senator Everett Dirksen probably didn't say. The point of all these taxes is to spread the pain so we notice it less. And, generally, that works. People have no idea how much tax they are actually suffering.

In accordance with the First Golden Rule, the sugar tax is a small impost added to the cost of soft drinks that are already subject to VAT. It's being introduced from April 2018 and will probably add 8p to the price of a can of Coca Cola. Although the sugar tax is supposed to fight obesity by making sugary drinks more expensive, it is not clear that the most effective way of doing so is with another tax and all the bureaucracy that goes with it.

The Second Golden Rule: No matter what name is on the bill, all taxes are ultimately suffered by human beings

Only people can pay taxes. As we saw in Chapter 1, employers' national insurance contributions are really a tax on our salaries, not a tax on our employers. And in Chapter 2, we discovered that, while VAT may be handed to the taxman by the businesses we buy stuff from, we end up paying all of it. Even corporation tax, which sounds like a tax on companies, is really suffered by shareholders, customers and staff.

The sugar tax is no exception. Consistent with the Second Golden Rule, it is levied on the manufacturers of sweetened drinks but they can be expected to pass the cost on to consumers by increasing the prices of their products. Indeed, they might increase the price of diet drinks in order to keep the cost of their sugary and non-sugary products the same.

The Third Golden Rule: Taxes are kept as invisible as possible

Since we all hate paying taxes, the government has perfected the art of ensuring that we rarely have to hand over the money ourselves. Most taxes are paid by businesses on our behalf. We've seen how the PAYE system hides how much national insurance and income tax we pay, while VAT and excise duty are buried in high-street prices. Environmental taxes on our energy bills are in deep cover and don't even admit to being taxes. To be honest, almost all taxes are stealth taxes.

We noted above that the sugar tax will be paid by drinks manufacturers but consumers will suffer the tax through higher prices. However, shoppers won't know how much soft drinks industry levy they are paying when they buy a sugary beverage. In fact, they are unlikely to be aware that they are paying it at all. Following the Third Golden Rule, it is kept under wraps.

The new Making Tax Digital initiative will remove us even further from the process by which we pay tax. As I mentioned in Chapter 1, HMRC wants to collect what's due on our savings through the PAYE machinery operated by employers. If the plan works, tax returns will be abolished within five years. Once that happens, the vast majority of the UK population will never have to think about tax again. It will represent the apotheosis of the Golden Rules of tax.

The Three Golden Rules explain why the tax system is organised the way it is. They are the reason we have so many taxes, why stealth taxes are so popular with governments, and why we rarely have to pay money directly to HMRC. The soft drinks industry levy complies with all three rules. This suggests to me that it is designed to raise extra revenue, even though the government claims it wants the levy to reduce sugar consumption. If that were the case, it would be better if the tax were highly visible so that shoppers could immediately see how much extra their sugar hit was costing them. We are warned about the 5p charge for plastic bags, introduced in October

2015, every time we buy a bag at the check-out. As a result, we have used billions fewer than we did before the 5p charge was introduced. If the government wants the soft drinks industry levy to change behaviour, it should defy the Golden Rules and make the tax as obvious as possible.

Lack of transparency is one reason that government attempts to use taxes to change behaviour are often ineffective. Another problem with tax incentives is that people take advantage of them in a way that governments didn't intend. Tax avoidance of this kind gives rise to lots of extra tax rules specifically to prevent it. And the unexpected consequences of anti-avoidance rules often provide new ways of avoiding taxes. This leads to even more intricacies as the authorities try to close down loopholes they accidentally created closing other loopholes. In addition, we have seen how tax reform often makes the law more elaborate as exceptions have to be made for those who would otherwise lose out from change.

This means there are sound political reasons why the tax system remains so complex, even though this complexity has real costs. Large companies regularly need to employ a dozen or more staff to keep track of all their tax obligations, while the fees for tax advice paid to the UK's biggest six accountancy firms are approaching a combined total of £3 billion a year. However, cries for simplification rarely explain how the challenges we noted above are supposed to be overcome. Academics and think tanks pontificate about radical flat taxes and land value imposts and basic incomes but, in the real world, these are non-starters. That's why, in this book, I haven't tried to sell you any of these hobbyhorses, however fine they might sound in theory.

Likewise, demands to tax high earners don't acknowledge how much we do that already. People with big salaries pay a large proportion of tax and it is unlikely we can squeeze a great deal more out of them. Admittedly, the independently wealthy are under-taxed and perhaps my suggestion for a minimum income tax rate of 30% might help. We've also seen that increasing corporation tax is economically unwise because it is effectively a tax on investment.

Company taxes should be low and straightforward, or they reward multinationals that arrange their affairs to circumvent them.

Political difficulties mean that comprehensive tax reform is unlikely. We're stuck with the arrangements we've got. Even tinkering around the edges is fraught with hazard, as George Osborne's 'omnishambles' budget of 2012 illustrated. His sensible package of moderate reforms became a presentational disaster. Another thing that isn't going to change is the answer to the question: who pays the tax in this country? The answer is you and me. The UK tax system is geared towards collecting income tax and national insurance contributions on our salaries, as well as VAT on the money we spend.

There are clear advantages to basing the tax system around income tax. We saw several in Chapter 1. It is easy to collect because most people are employed. Through PAYE, the costs of administering tax collection are borne by employers and the government skims off its share when our salary is paid over to us. We don't even see most of the tax we pay. This makes avoiding income tax and national insurance almost impossible, at least without the connivance of our employers. Income tax is broad-based and the majority of people have to pay something. It can also be skewed towards the wealthiest. As we saw in Chapter 1, the so-called 1%, the best paid people in the country, pay 25% of all income tax. So the system is 'progressive' in that high earners pay progressively more as they get better off. VAT is also administered by businesses. The ordinary people who pay it when they buy something don't have to deal with HMRC.

The problem with taxing us lot, the voters, is that we have votes. We can turn the government out of office if it increases our taxes by more than we will bear. That we don't do so more often is a tribute to the ingenuity of a system that can extract billions without us even noticing. Since the only people who will pay our taxes are us, we might as well be more vocal in demanding value for our money when the government spends it.

I hope, after reading this book, you are more aware of just how much tax you pay. Just as importantly, I want to have persuaded you that, with taxation, there are no easy answers.

Index

Printed and bound by CPI Group (UK) Ltd, Croydon, CR0 4YY
26/01/2022

03106291-0001